There is Still More.

REACHING FOR MORE OF THE KINGDOM

Mar

RIVER
PUBLISHING

River Publishing & Media Ltd
Barham Court
Teston
Maidstone
Kent
ME18 5BZ
United Kingdom

info@river-publishing.co.uk

ISBN 978-1-908393-03-6

Printed in the United Kingdom

Contents

Preface

Once more I have put pen to paper, hopefully not to bore people, but to inspire us all to stretch for more of what God has for us. As I have reflected on my life I have been amazed at God's goodness and constancy through the years and it has been a profitable exercise to chronicle some of what God has done. This has encouraged me and I pray it might be an encouragement to others to press in for still more.

As always I have to thank my ever patient husband, David, who has read the manuscript and suggested grammatical and spelling alterations. I thank my friends Anderly in Chile and Prue just up the road, who have both read parts of the manuscript and given me their honest critique. What would we do without friends! Also Tim Pettingale has given invaluable advice and help.

I was encouraged to write this, yet another book, first by David, but also by John Coles and Phil George. The latter two have given me that little extra push to attempt another DVD or to write another book. Without their encouragement I would, most likely, be vegetating and letting my brain grow idle.

Ever since I read Catherine Marshall's book *Something More*, I have wanted to write something similar. That book inspired me, with each chapter being based on a different aspect of the Christian life. It was so easy to read, especially because it was so full of her own experiences and the lessons she had learned through them. Though obviously very different in content, I have followed her format and based each chapter on events in my own life.

My prayer is that something within these pages will help and bless all who read it.

Mary Pytches,
May 2011

1
Can I Ask
For More?

In the spring of 2010, before the New Wine summer conference, I was asked what seminar I would like to do. I felt it was far too early for me to make a decision like that and for the life of me I couldn't imagine what I might want to speak about in four month's time. But after pondering the problem I decided that I would like to do a seminar entitled, "There is Still More" – a title that gave me the freedom to speak on just about anything! However, another problem soon arose when I was asked to write a short summary of what the seminar would be about. What "more" was I going to speak about? So this is what I wrote:

"Paul wrote to the Philippians that he was straining towards what lay ahead. Whatever stage we have reached in our Christian life there is always more to discover and experience. Are you hungry to experience more of the treasures of the kingdom? Then together we will look at some of the joys God has in store for us as well as some of the challenges."

This left me free to enjoy sharing whatever might be on my heart when the time came.

However, before I sat down to prepare, I had to reassure myself that asking for more was permissible. When Oliver Twist had the audacity to ask for more of the thin gruel that was the staple diet of the Parish Workhouse, of which he was an unhappy inmate, he was locked up and a notice was posted outside the gate offering a reward of five pounds to anyone who would take Oliver Twist off the hands of the Parish. His daring request was considered out of order. It was made to appear that Oliver had committed an unforgivable sin.

Even at the girl's boarding school I attended for seven years we were never permitted to ask for more, or for anything we needed at the meal table, unless someone else first invited us to have some salt, butter or whatever. I'm afraid the result was a few bruised ankles. In many circles asking for more is considered rude or greedy.

Some would even say that it is bad theology to want more. Don't we have it "all" in Christ already anyway? Potentially, I believe we do. But most of us don't enjoy the riches which are ours by right as children of God. We are rather like a millionaire who lives a meagre existence instead of enjoying the plenty that he could well afford. On the back page of the book *More* by Simon Ponsonby, someone has written, "Simon Ponsonby explores the wonderful paradox that, even though we 'have it all' in Christ, there is more to enjoy." Watchman Nee, a well known 20th century Christian leader in China, put it this way: "Our own grasp of Him and of His work can grow. *He changes not.*"[1]

I had been a Christian sixteen years before I experienced an anointing, a touch, a filling or maybe some would call it a "baptism" of the Holy Spirit. I know that I already had the Spirit or I wouldn't have been able to declare, "Jesus is Lord".[2] Nevertheless, what I experienced on that occasion was something I had never experienced before and to my surprise opened the door to much more than I anticipated — such as speaking in tongues, a greater love for the word of God and for Jesus and a joy that was indescribable. I had previously considered myself a conservative evangelical, and still do, but my friends were very sceptical of the charismatic renewal that was taking place all over the world. However, from one moment to the next I had joined the ranks of those whom I had previously considered "over the top" and "unbiblical". I had distrusted the talk of supernatural gifts and the show of emotion in worship. I thought that it was just not for me. At first I didn't give my experience a name. I wasn't sure what had happened exactly. I just knew that I had begged God to do something new in my life and He had! To this day, forty years later, I am extremely grateful that God heard my prayer and answered as He did. I have experienced more than I ever dreamt was possible and it has continued year after year. God has repeatedly surprised me with more glimpses of His kingdom. And I am assured there is "more" yet to come.

Fortunately, the Bible is full of encouragements to enjoy a huge variety of "more" that is on offer. Jesus clearly told us to, *"Ask and it will be given you ... for everyone who asks receives."*[3] It would seem that God wants us to be hungry and thirsty Christians. For example, take the statement that Jesus made to His disciples when they asked Him to explain the parable of the Sower. He said, *"Whoever has will be given **more**, and he will have an abundance."*[4] And when Paul prayed for the Philippians he asked that their love might abound more and more in knowledge and depth of insight. Paul also encourages the Ephesian Christians to become more mature, *"attaining to the whole measure of the* *fullness of Christ."*[5] Just from those few verses it would seem clear that there are more challenges, more riches to experience and more understanding of the kingdom to enjoy now and in the life to come.

I gave my first ever real "talk" aged twenty-one when I was at Bible College. It was based on Paul's letter to the Corinthians where he writes about his hardships and ends with the words, *"...as having nothing and yet possessing all things."*[6] It was a fascinating thought. I knew that, materially, my husband to be and I possessed very little. We had offered ourselves to the mission field and once married anticipated that that was where we would soon be heading. The pay would be enough to feed us, but without any of the luxuries we had presumed were necessary to life, such as butter, sweets, ice cream, etc. In fact, even cheese would be scarce. Holidays would depend on other people's generosity and living accommodation would be basic and most likely shared. We would be living on the bare necessities. But that verse gave me much food for thought. I was a relatively new Christian and had been tested very little, but I trusted that God would provide all that we needed. I had a feeling that the future held an extraordinary adventure, where I would be able to experience the "all things" that Paul wrote about.

Our story is not exceptional. David and I are both very ordinary people as our families would be quick to point out. We are definitely far from perfect.

However, the content of the seminar at New Wine which I eventually gave was largely drawn from my own journey and what I had learned through both the good and bad times. In particular, I wanted to share what had proved helpful to me and might therefore be of benefit to others. I enjoyed the seminar and wished the time had allowed for more, which is partly why I decided to write this, yet another book, where I could enlarge on the subject of "there is still more".

Several people have suggested I write a biography. David has already written an account of our life called *Living at the Edge*, and I have no desire to add to that. But nevertheless, one learns many lessons through life's ups and downs and I have purposely drawn from those experiences throughout this book. The first book I wrote, back in the early eighties, was very short and to the point. My publisher, the late Edward England, commented that he didn't find "me" in the pages of the book. I hadn't intended that he should. But this time, were he alive, he would probably say there was too much of me! I apologise if that offends!

Endnotes:

1. *A Table in the Wilderness*, daily mediations from the ministry of Watchman Nee
2. 1 Corinthians 12:3
3. Luke 11:9
4. Matthew 13:12
5. Ephesians 4:13
6. 2 Corinthians 6:10

2
Amazed By God's Purposes

When I left school at seventeen I had no idea of what I wanted to do with my life. I had done well in the subjects that had interested me, but Sport, English and History didn't seem to point towards a particular career. I had been popular with my fellow students, but I was definitely not a favourite with the staff. I seemed incapable of keeping out of trouble and had quickly earned the reputation of being a rebel. In the end, the headmistress politely wrote to my parents and told them I was too old for school and needed to leave. I think the school had wearied of trying to contain me. So then the problem belonged to my parents and eventually they decided to send me to live with Ruby, one of my married sisters, in Oxford where I could attend a local Secretarial College.

I was delighted to be free from school and to be in a place swarming with so many interesting young men. "Miss Sprules Academy for Young Ladies" was, in effect, an old fashioned type of finishing school where they prepared young ladies to become

PA's to "important" people. I quickly decided that was not for me. But I quite enjoyed the novelty of learning typing and shorthand and, to my surprise, discovered that I was good at administration – so the course was not a total waste of time. One of the things impressed upon us was that we should consider our first job as part of our training and not something we would necessarily enjoy – and that we should aim to stay in it for at least a year, after which time it would be fine to look for something more to our liking. So after six months of college I began to search the local newspaper and found myself a job in the local tax office. I was placed in the PAYE department.

Nothing could have been more unsuitable! I have no head for figures and the job was mostly typing cheques and letters about money. My boss was a bad tempered man who seemed to have lost the ability ever to smile. He treated me as a "non-person" who was there for his convenience. When he needed to see me he would ring a bell which sounded in our office. For some reason it didn't suit him to give one short ring. Instead, it was like a fire alarm which continued to ring until I appeared at his office door, out of breath and so nervous that I was incapable of writing in shorthand something that I could later decipher!

I shared an office with two other women – one about my age and another who was older. She would sit enveloped in a cloud of cigarette smoke, her eyes screwed up as she tried to read her notes through the haze, and her two fingers racing across the keyboard at an incredible speed. I remember her being a very kind person who frequently rescued me from the mistakes I made in those early weeks.

To begin with, the environment felt foreign to me, coming as I had from a rather small, elite boarding school and a definitely "up-market" secretarial college. I was unprepared for the real world of ordinary people. I hated it all. The job bored me, my boss scared me, and I didn't know how to relate to my office companions. The lack of meaning and purpose in my life depressed me. I frequently questioned what life was all about and could not come up with an answer that satisfied me.

Victor Frankl, a survivior of the holocaust wrote, "This striving to find a meaning to one's life is the primary motivational force in man."[1] Certainly without recognising it, I was on a search for a reason as to why I had been put on this planet.

The weekends were my escape. By this time I had moved out of my sister's house to the local YWCA hostel. It was cheap and I met some interesting people there. Saturday afternoon was spent washing clothes and getting ready for whatever party was on the agenda that evening. Then I would spend Sunday morning recovering from the night before. In the afternoon we would often sit around the lounge having discussions about life. In the evening my friend, with whom I shared a room, and I would take off to a local cinema. It helped me to avoid thinking about the next day, knowing that once again I would have to face that dreaded office.

In those Sunday afternoon discussions I always took the stance of an agnostic. My family had not been church goers, but they were good people whom I would describe as God-fearing. I'd had an introduction to Christianity during school assemblies and from the High Anglican church we attended on Sunday mornings during term time.

All I remember about those services was counting the cricket score as the priest waved his arms around during the sermon. My childhood experience of church left me unconvinced about Christianity. I thought there was probably a God, but as far as I could tell, He was not in the slightest bit interested in me and therefore had no bearing on my life.

However, some of the girls in the hostel were Christians and one of them was quite persistent in her arguments with me. One day this particular girl presented me with an official looking invitation to a visitor's service at her church. Out of boredom and having nothing better on offer, I agreed to go with her. When the time came I regretted my decision because my roommate, a minister's daughter, was adamant that any film whatsoever would be preferable to going to church. But I felt committed to the previous invitation. The standards by which I lived my life were largely left over from my boarding school days and I knew that in their book a commitment was a commitment. So I kept my promise to go and got ready for a boring evening.

The church was tucked away in a back street near the centre of Oxford. It was small and cosy and had a very peaceful feel to it. I sat there while Evensong sort of washed over me. The clergyman preached on Jesus standing outside the door of my heart and wanting to come in and have a relationship with me. It touched a part of me that I didn't know existed and I was sorely tempted to respond to the invitation to go forward, but I was not quite ready to take such an important step.

But the whole service had had the effect of allaying my anxiety and lifting my depression. I secretly made a decision to come back each week, just to take away a little of the peace I had enjoyed there. I thought it might get me through the week ahead.

After the service had ended the girl who had taken me said she was going on to a meeting of University students and asked, would I like to go with her? Always up for something with students present I agreed. It turned out to be the Fresher's meeting run by the Oxford Intervarsity Christian Union. To my amazement, a different clergyman spoke on exactly the same verse I had already heard in the little church.

I felt spooked but at the same time excited, and without any hesitation I went forward at the end of the evening as a sign that I wanted to become a Christian. I was by now convinced that this was the answer to my search. The preacher's name was Maurice Wood who was later to become the Bishop of Norwich.

I walked home in a daze and woke up the next morning – the dreaded Monday – and nothing seemed to have changed. I would be catching the bus to the office, which would still be dealing in taxes, and work for a boss who would still be bad tempered, in an office still filled with smoke.

But in fact, everything had changed. That morning I awoke knowing, without a shadow of doubt, that my life now had meaning. I was sure that everything I did from then on would have a purpose to it. I couldn't have told anyone what that purpose was exactly, but it completely changed my attitude – to the bus ride, to the office, to my boss and to my fellow workers. I believed that God had put me in that place for a reason which filled me with excitement and anticipation. I could hardly wait to get to the office and share my story with whoever would listen.

From that day on I found my life has had meaning to it – in more amazing ways than I ever imagined. Through all the ups and downs of over fifty years of following Christ, this has been one of the main things to sustain me. I think Dallas Willard hit the nail on the head when he wrote,

"Meaning is not a luxury for us. It is a kind of spiritual oxygen, we might say, that enables our souls to live."[2]

When we can find no meaning in our lives it drives us into depression and maybe it's one of the main factors why many of our young people are ruining their lives with sex, alcohol and drugs. Again Willard writes, "Meaning nourishes our soul. It is one of the greatest human needs, one of our deepest hungers – perhaps the most basic human need ... Meaning can make pain and exertion, tedium and sorrow not only bearable but even exhilarating."[3]

Certainly, since becoming a Christian, the tedium of office life had become more than bearable and later, the challenges and problems that inevitably arise in life, were sustainable. My sense of purpose had a definite bearing on being able to rise above the storms of life. One of the discoveries Victor Frankl made while cruelly incarcerated was that those who had a reason to live were more likely to survive the atrocities they experienced at the hands of the Nazis.

As the years have progressed, I have come to a relatively simple conclusion as to the reason for our sojourn on this earth. The primary purpose God has for each of us does not take a great intellect to discover. It isn't rocket science. As with most things in the Christian life, it is simple enough for the least educated to understand and complex enough for the greatest intellect.

Why did God create man in the first place? From the first chapter of Genesis we see that God lived in community with the Son and the Holy Spirit. After creating the world and populating it with fish, birds and animals He says, *"Let us make man in our own image, in our likeness..."*[4] The Trinity who dwelt in fellowship then created humankind in their likeness and with the ability to share in that fellowship.

As one early mystic put it, "we were created out of the laughter of the Trinity."[5] Later we find God walking in the garden in the cool of the day and looking for Adam and Eve. *"Where are you?"*[6] He calls. Such a personal question. But man's disobedience had caused him to hide from that relationship. It had interrupted the open communication between God and man. Yet God had not finished with humankind. He planned a rescue mission which culminated in the coming of Jesus.

When God created Adam and Eve we read that He blessed them and then sent them out to rule over His creation.[7] Later we read that God had a similar purpose for Abraham, who had been called from Ur of the Chaldeans to enter the Promised Land. God said,

"I will make you into a great nation and I will **bless you**; I will make your name great and you will be a **blessing**. I will bless those who bless you and whoever curses you I will curse; and **all the peoples of the earth will be blessed through you**."[8] The purposes of God are fulfilled within a relationship of intimacy in which we are blessed by Him. When children were blessed by their fathers they received it in their father's presence. When Isaac blessed Jacob, thinking he was Esau, he did it when Jacob came into his presence pretending to be his brother.[9] When Jacob blessed Joseph's sons, Ephraim and Manasseh, they came into his presence where he could touch them.

This is God's principal purpose in creating us – for relationship. It's our primary calling. As someone has said, "We have been called into a 'Cosmic Love Affair' of immense proportions." This and only this will provide us with the purpose and meaning that our souls need. God has designed us for intimacy with Himself and without it our lives will lose their bearing. Nothing will ever make any real sense. Yet it is so easy to get diverted. Having prayed with many people over the years and knowing the waywardness of my own heart, I am aware of how easy it is to get caught up in our own petty dramas and miss the greatest drama of all time.

When we stray back into our own "story" and miss God's greater story it can seem so reasonable. For example, when we feel overlooked or unappreciated it is easy to become focused on the unfairness of the situation and lose sight of the fact that life is not just about us. We have been called to live our lives in the greatest story of all time. It's all about the love of God and His amazing kingdom – not about us. But Satan would have us think that we are the main players and should have special treatment.

In the story of Pilgrims Progress, By-Path Meadow was a lush field very near a difficult place on the way to the Celestial City. Christian was enticed into taking the easy way. It was a diversion that he soon regretted for Giant Despair roamed there. He was caught and cast into the dungeon of Doubting Castle.

By-Path Meadow has many names and is ruled over by our enemy, Satan, with our particular weaknesses in mind. His major goal is to distract us from the greater purposes of God and in particular from intimacy with God, and we convince ourselves that his suggestions are sensible and attractive. If we want to experience more of God, then, we need to be intentional about seeking His presence.

Endnotes:

1. Frankl, Victor, *Man's Search for Meaning,* Rider, 2004.

2. Willard, Dallas, *The Divine Conspiracy*, Fount, 1998.

3. Willard, Dallas, *Renovations of the Heart*, IVP, 2002.

4. Genesis 1:26

5. Curtis, Brent and Eldredge, John, *The Sacred Romance*, Thomas Nelson Publishers, 1997.

6. Genesis 3:9

7. Genesis 3.28

8. Genesis 12:2

9. Genesis 27

3
Diversions

After I had been a Christian a couple of weeks the Rector of the church, St Ebbes, Oxford, where I had started attending invited me to coffee. The Rev Basil Gough listened to my story and then asked me if there were any questions I wanted to ask him. I would like to have produced a deep theological problem, but the only thing that came into my mind was the party I had promised to attend the following evening. I had arranged to go with the latest boyfriend, but my instinct told me that it might not be the most suitable environment, now that I had become a Christian. However, I had made a commitment and wasn't sure how I could get out of it at this late hour.

Basil's response was memorable. He was rather an other-worldly sort of man. In fact, I later learned that one of his heroes was the very saintly Bishop Hanley Moule, who once attended a football match in Durham and when his side scored was reputed to have thrown his hat in the air and exclaimed, "Ooh, what an abundantly blessed goal!" It struck me that Basil would probably have done likewise. In fact, I would not have been surprised if Basil had given me some "other-worldly" advice. Instead it was very practical – far from what I imagined coming from him. Having thought for a moment, he suggested that the best way forward was to take Jesus with me to the party. What a novel idea! But the more I thought about it the more right it appeared.

So the next evening I knelt by my bed before leaving to meet the unsuspecting young man and asked Jesus to accompany me to the party. As I had thought, the party began to degenerate by about midnight. The lights went out and couples were disappearing into various corners of the house. My friend was beginning to get restless and began the usual advances, hoping to elicit a response from me. Not getting what he expected he asked me what was wrong.

I remember sitting on his knee and asking him, "What would you think if Jesus walked into the room right now?" His immediate response was to push me off, leap out of the chair and exclaim, "Oh my ...! Let's get out of here."

We spent the next few hours walking the streets of Oxford while I shared my story. I never saw him again, but I heard that for the next few days I was the topic of conversation at his college. Basil's simple words have stayed with me ever since and I have often passed his advice on to others.

My family were worried that I had become a religious fanatic. What I failed to get across to them was that it wasn't about religion, it was about a relationship.

However, Oxford was a city of many distractions and in those early days I found myself frequently getting drawn away from my primary calling into some second-best relationship which I thought would satisfy me. Our basic needs, the three "S's", as

Selwyn Hughes used to call them, are very demanding and it is easy to get trapped into thinking that our drive for meaning and purpose will be met when those needs are satisfied.

One of those needs is *significance* – the desire to do something that meets the need to be appreciated, to be needed, to feel important, to be mentally stimulated and to be successful. Then there's *self-worth* – the need to be valued for myself, not just for what I do or to whom I am attached, but just because I am me. And lastly there is *security* – the need to be loved, to have our emotional needs met, to have the future mapped out, a place to live, to have financial security and to feel safe.

The pressure to meet those needs could easily cause any one of us to be diverted into By-Path Meadow. And Satan is constantly beckoning us in that direction. Then, as Curtis and Eldredge aptly explain, we get caught up in our mini -stories and miss the "Mega-Story".

When Jesus told the story of the prodigal son,[1] He didn't explain the reasons behind the young man's journey into the far country, but he probably didn't feel that his needs were being met at home. He foolishly ran from the place where he belonged, where he was known – the place where he could be loved and supported – for the imagined attractions, excitement and freedom of the far country. Home can sometimes seem dull, unexciting and not what we feel satisfies us any longer.

A few weeks ago I read a book entitled, *So You Don't Want to go to Church Anymore*.[2] The author points out the imperfections of many of our churches, but instead of explaining why, with all their faults, they are vital to our lives, he justifies the reasons why so many younger Christians have given up on the organised Church and prefer to meet occasionally in the local pub or where ever. In fact, the author no longer goes to any church himself. Then during the summer at the New Wine conference I heard a young man, James Mumford, speak on, "Why I go to church religiously – the beauty of banality". He spelt out the reasons why he might decide not to go to either his church or his small group, but then explained the absolute necessity of belonging to them. There is no perfect church because there are no perfect Christians, but it is what Jesus ordained and we have to keep doing all we can to improve it.

I started attending the church I was first taken to and was convinced that if I was to stay a Christian I had to make new friends there. But it proved harder than I imagined. I am reasonably outgoing and friendly and have never had a problem getting to know people. But, though no one said anything, I still felt like an outsider. It took me about a month before I tumbled as to the reason why. I didn't look like them! I wore jewellery, bright clothes, high heeled shoes and, worst of all, make-up! Eventually I gave in and conformed. Within a week I was asked to be the secretary of the Young People's Fellowship. I was in! That is not how it is in every church, but was the way it seemed to me in my new family of the Church at the time.

However many flaws the church may have we need to be part of it. It is where we can be known, supported and loved. I am eternally grateful to that little church. It taught me so much and gave me a wonderful biblical basis for the Christian faith.

Yes, it seemed legalistic in some ways; yes, it could be boring at times; yes, there was a degree of pride in their adherence to a standard of behaviour which other churches in the city didn't appear to adhere to – but it was part of the Church that Jesus founded and we leave it at our peril. John Wimber, the founder of the Vineyard movement, used to say that, "We must love the whole Church. The Church is not our enemy, Satan is."

Looking back, it was that group of slightly legalistic Christians that I kept returning to from my occasional detours and with whom I found myself growing steadily in faith and in my relationship to God. It was in that church that I was first challenged about becoming a missionary.

In the story of the Prodigal, the young man didn't just run away from his home. He was trying to run away from himself. I wonder if he had been treated like the baby of the family, or maybe he felt second best to his dutiful older brother?

It seemed that he may have been looking for a new and more significant identity and, for a while, in the far country he imagined he had found one. He became the popular, cool guy, the one to know, and he was surrounded with friends ... until his money ran out. Then he found himself not just "second best", but disillusioned, alone and a total failure.

The urge for significance can be very pressing and can cause us to take major detours like the prodigal, though they usually turn out to be short-lived and uncertain. In the end, the only identity that is secure, unchanging and totally satisfying is that found in our intimacy with God the Father and in who we are in Christ.

I was born the fourth child of rather elderly parents. My mother would sometimes introduce me as "my little accident" or "our little mistake"! It was never said with a desire to hurt. In fact, it was a bit of a family joke.

In some ways it was good to feel I had a different identity from my siblings. Nevertheless, something negative had embedded itself in my subconscious and I often found myself feeling as if I was a bit of an inconvenience, or needed a gold lettered invitation to visit someone in their home. I had been a Christian for many years before that misconception was challenged.

I was reading my Bible one night before going to sleep when a sentence jumped out at me. *"Therefore, as God's chosen people, holy and dearly loved..."*[3] "Chosen ... I have been chosen," I repeated to myself. Slowly, a truth I had known for many years moved from my head to my heart. Not only was I chosen, but I was dearly loved. What a fantastic identity. It was true that my mother was surprised at finding herself pregnant again, and in her eyes I might have been "a mistake".

But from the moment of reading those words I knew that I had been no mistake. God had purposed for me to be born. I almost felt as though I shared a secret joke with God. Of course, I still have a choice every day of my life to walk in the identity that God has given me that will endure for all eternity, or I could choose to walk in the old one I felt branded with all those years ago, and which will only survive the duration of my earthly life.

The prodigal eventually came home and discovered that he was a forgiven, dearly loved son of his father. That is the only identity, in the end, that will meet our need for significance.

Another thing that can cause us to take a trip into By-Path Meadow is our relationships. The older brother appeared to be a difficult, uptight young man; their personality differences must have made living together hard.

During our seventeen years in Chile we were frequently called upon to share our accommodation with other missionaries. After a few weeks, people's different ways of living, of dealing with problems, and in particular with children, took their toll on us. At times it seemed almost unbearable. God didn't make us carbon copies – we are all distinctive human beings!

I remember once complaining to one of our missionary nurses that the couple we were sharing our home with at the time made such a fuss about, what I considered, small things. If the wife hurt herself, the whole street knew about it and the husband appeared to go along with it. The nurse explained to me that we all have different pain thresholds and this particular woman had a very low one.

It helped at the time, but after about three months with this particular couple I remember feeling that I would have a nervous breakdown if I had to share our home with them for much longer. I have often derived comfort from some words of St Paul that my husband sometimes quotes (as an excuse for change!): *"So when we could stand it no longer..."*[4]

I had reached breaking point so David pulled out all the stops and found the other couple alternative accommodation. Thankfully we parted amicably and have remained friends ever since. As soon as there was some distance between us and we each had our own space we got on very well, and in fact, I was able to laugh at our differences. It may not always be possible to work at close quarters with some Christians, but that doesn't mean that we stop loving one another and can't find a way to remain in fellowship.

One of the churches in our region of Chile was located on a housing estate and it started in the house of a lady who had moved there from our church in the city. Eventually, the church was able to buy land and build their own worship centre. The lady still played a prominent role in the church, but she kept falling out with her neighbour, another member of the same church.

On one of his pastoral visits she complained to David saying that this woman was impossible to get on with and that she wasn't going to try any longer. So David asked if she had made her bed that morning? She was quite indignant and said that of course she had. Then he asked her if she had made it the day before? Again she replied, more indignantly still, that she had.

"Well why did you make the bed again if you had already done it the day before?" he asked her.

"Because it got unmade," she replied.

"Well," he said, "it is the same with relationships. They may get unmade and we just go on trying to make them up."

Of course, we will have times when relationships with others are difficult and we won't always see eye to eye. But we just have to forgive and then find a way of remaining in fellowship. If not, we could easily find ourselves in the far country.

The young prodigal eventually came home and discovered the huge mercy and love of his father. How healing that embrace must have been. But the story doesn't end there, because a celebration was called for and in the last part of the story the focus is on the older brother who refuses to join in. It would seem that he was in By-Path Meadow and didn't realise it.

His problem was that he had a wrong perception, both of himself and of his father. The older brother had not taken a physical journey from home, but an emotional one. Just as the younger brother had "come to himself" and rethought his position, so the older brother needed to have his eyes opened to his irrational thinking which was keeping him from intimacy with his father.

He saw himself as more trustworthy and hardworking and, because of that, much more deserving of his father's favours than his young brother. He saw his father as unfair.

Of all the detours we can take from intimacy this is perhaps the most dangerous. It is so easy to be there week by week in God's presence, working hard and doing all the right things, yet missing God's primary call to intimacy with Him.

It is so easy to slip into "doing for God", which seems so right and at the same time feeds our self-image, instead of just being thankful that we are God's chosen, beloved children with no sense of obligation to earn that position. The call on our lives has an order to it: *being* before *doing*.

Once we have that right, our "doing" will be coming from the right place.

Intimacy might be our primary call, and the major thing to give meaning to our lives, yet there are other reasons why we may miss it, which we will look at in the next chapter.

Endnotes:

1. Luke 15:8
2. Jacobsen, Wayne and Coleman, Dave, So You Don't Want to go to Church Anymore, Faith Words, 2008.
3. Colossians 3:12
4. 1 Thessalonians 3:1

4
More Diversions

I grew up in a village in North Devon. I was the youngest of four – three girls and a boy. Both my parents worked in the family business and I was therefore left a great deal to my own devices and mainly looked after by my older sisters. I knew that I was loved – that was never in doubt – but I did wonder sometimes whether my father, a good man who worked hard to provide for his family, was particularly interested in me. He was a very quiet man and I don't remember ever having a meaningful conversation with him.

At the time it didn't bother me. It was just how it was. It was only years later when I struggled, feeling a sense of distance from God the Father, that I joined up the dots. I knew Jesus was my friend and saviour who was with me and with whom I had a relationship, but God the Father seemed a distant, slightly impersonal part of the Trinity. When I understood how easy it is to see God through the lens of our own experience, I began to work on my attitude to Him, as my Heavenly Father.

The story of the Prodigal Son, as it is popularly called, is really a story that Jesus told to show us the mercy, compassion and constant concern His Heavenly Father has for His children. So I spent some time changing my perception of fathering, as I had experienced it, to the picture Jesus gives us of His Heavenly Father throughout the gospels.

It changed not just how I felt about God the Father, but how I felt about myself. I often tell people that comparing God the Father to our own earthly fathers is like comparing the light of the sun with the light of a candle. Both are lights, but that is where the comparison ends. However, many people miss out on the relationship God has called us to for this simple reason – misconceptions about God the Father.

In his book, *The Singing God*, Sam Storms recounts a pastoral encounter he had with a young girl he calls Susan. Susan was hospitalised with an emotional breakdown and Sam visited her there. Her father had been a demanding tyrant who dangled his love over Susan like a carrot. "If you are good ... pretty ... clever etc ... I will love you."

But Susan never measured up. She was never good enough, pretty enough or clever enough for her father. Sam tried desperately to minister the love of God to her, but she could not begin to see God as her loving Father and could not receive His love.

One day Sam asked her a question: "What does God feel about you?"

"Pity", Susan replied without hesitation.

"Why?" Sam asked her.

"Because I am pitiful and I'm pathetic."

For a further hour Sam tried to make Susan see how much God loved her, but to no avail. Then he asked her to read Zephaniah chapter 3 and verse 17.

"The Lord your God is with you, he is mighty to save. He will take great delight in you, he will quiet you with his love. He will rejoice over you with singing."

Susan read it aloud and was stunned. "God sings? God sings over me?"

After a few moments of shocked silence tears began to well up in her eyes and stream down her face. "Sam, are you sure?" she asked. Again Sam got her to read the passage. The tears returned. "If only I could believe it were true. I think then I could face almost anything. If only it were true."[1]

If only it were true!

So often I found myself knowing many wonderful truths about God with my mind, but they never seemed to penetrate to my heart. God longs to have a relationship with us. It is His primary purpose in creating us and yet we have so often been sidetracked or missed it for one reason or another. Susan was missing it because she was still struggling with emotional blockages due to the poor fathering.

We live in a very broken world where love can be dished out in a conditional manner, as it was for Susan. Even though no one may have intentionally said it to us, we can so easily pick up a message that was never intended.

A friend of mine was struggling with a very difficult job and came to talk about giving it up. I knew she was quite capable of doing the work, but fear of failure was blocking her from wanting to try. She had never failed at anything in her life and though I felt it was very unlikely, it suddenly seemed to her to be a distinct possibility.

Her family had always praised her and been delighted by her achievements, but somewhere a thought had crept in: "What if I fail? Would they still be pleased with me?" Gradually, her fear of possible failure grew until she was paralysed by the thought.

Twisted thinking, misconceptions and misunderstandings are all part and parcel of living in a fallen world. In our broken society where love is so often conditional, it is hard to imagine that God loves us unconditionally. Many of us, like Susan, do not see ourselves as loveable. How do we remedy this?

First, we need to understand the heart of a Creator. When we create something, however small, it gives us pleasure. It may be a flower arrangement, a painting, a piece of furniture, a garden, a poem. Whatever it is, when we have given birth to it we derive immense satisfaction from it and want to protect it.

I remember when my husband David wrote his memoirs, the publisher wanted to cut it down and leave out some of his childhood recollections. David said to me that he couldn't do it. "Someone else would have to do it. For me to do it would be like cutting the ears off my own baby," he said.

God saw His creation, of which we were the culmination, and He saw that it was *very good*.[2] Looking up the Hebrew for "very good" I found that "very" could be translated as "exceedingly or utterly" and "good" as "best, precious, pleasing or beautiful". So when God looks at us He sees us as, "exceedingly and utterly precious, pleasing and beautiful". It literally couldn't be better!

Secondly, we need to try and understand the heart of a perfect father. Most parents love their children. They may not be able to show it very well, but they love them. I realised how much my own, very undemonstrative father, loved me when I was told how upset he had been because my cousin from Swansea had passed on diphtheria to me. Apparently, he refused to invite them ever to come and stay at our home after that. Though sadly it was unforgiving of my father, nevertheless it sent me a message that he really cared about me.

Another problem we may have is seeing ourselves as we really are, so far removed from our original creation. We think of who God is – the God who created the universe, a God of awesome power and dazzling purity – then we try to imagine God loving us, the sorry sight that we are. Though it is true that we are like damaged goods, that doesn't stop God loving us. Most human parents don't stop loving their children, even when they mess up. They might drive us to distraction, but they are still our kids!

After we retired from St Andrew's, Chorleywood in 1996, David and I began attending a Youth church in Watford run by our one time youth leader, Mike Pilavachi. Soul Survivor numbered probably about fifty people at that time and we were by far the oldest there. One young couple, originally from our church in Chorleywood, had moved with Mike at the birth of the church. They were the first to start a family. It was a great moment for the church when our first baby was born. She was the sweetest baby – blond and blue eyed. She began to grow into a gorgeous, friendly, bonny baby.

But then she never seemed to want to do anything but sit and hold out her arms to whoever would give her a kiss and a hug. Crawling did not happen. Eventually the doctors did some investigations and the parents were given the shattering news that little Ruthie had "Angel syndrome" – so called because the sufferers are the most loving, attractive people. Ruthie will probably never speak, nor walk without aid, but does that mean that her Mother and Father have stopped loving her or the church family for that matter. Never! She is adored by all. However imperfect or broken we may be, God has never stopped loving us.

Another block to some of us is accepting that if God loves us so passionately, it must mean that God is emotional. Most Westerners are sickened by sentimentality and feel uncomfortable when there is too much emotion around. We imagine a God who is in control – the strong silent type. But God's song in Zephaniah is not "emotionalism". It is full of emotion, yes, but not the manipulated, whipped-up sort that makes most of us recoil. The prophet reveals that God has strong feelings expressed in an emotional way.

He also writes of God's wrath and jealousy.[3] John tells us that God so loved the world that He was prepared to give His own son for it.[4] In Luke's gospel we read that Jesus saw Jerusalem and wept over it.[5] Mark writes of Jesus' righteous anger when He drives the money changers out of the temple.[6] And then there is what to my mind is the saddest verse in the Bible: *"I thought you would call me Father and not turn away from following me."*[7] We could list many more expressions of emotion. But in the third chapter of Zephaniah it is the love, care and joy of a parent that is being expressed.

"He will take great delight in you. He will quiet you with his love, He will rejoice over you with singing."[8]

When our first baby was born, she was very small and colicky. I had been quite ill having her and so David became a very "hands-on" Dad. I shall never forget him walking up and down the bedroom rocking this tiny baby and singing psalms over her. I am sure her amazing ear for music came from this time. He thought she was the best thing since sliced bread and no time spent with her seemed too much. He definitely quietened her with his love.

The picture we get from Zephaniah is of God like a father with his newborn baby. He is filled with joy and can hardly contain himself. The primitive root for the Hebrew word "rejoice" is to "twirl around". God is so delighted with us that He "twirls around with glee". And when we are sad or lonely, when our hearts yearn for love, we can take comfort from this verse and allow God to quiet us with great tenderness.

Of everything I have ever learned about God; of everything

I have ever spoken about, this is, to my mind, one of the most important of all the truths in the Bible. God created us for Himself – before anything and everyone else – for Himself. That is our primary call – to intimacy with the God who created us and loves us passionately. As Oz Guinness, in his wonderful book *The Call* writes,

"First and foremost we are called to Someone (God), not to something (such as motherhood, politics or teaching), or to somewhere (such as the inner city or Outer Mongolia)."[9] This is our secondary call – the call to go. In the Covenant God made with Abraham, He first blessed his people and then sent them out to be a blessing.

*"I will make you into a great nation and I will bless you; I will make your name great and you will be a blessing. I will bless those who bless you and whoever curses you I will curse and **all the peoples of the earth will be blessed through you**."*[10]

We need to be marinated with God's blessing and that only happens in God's presence. When we are blessed so much we won't be able to help but be a blessing wherever we go. It reminds me of a story told by CS Lewis in his book *The Great Divorce*.[11] The theme is about a bus journey from Hell to the outskirts of Heaven, where the travellers are given an opportunity to make different choices. There was doubt that one lady still had the power to choose because she had spent her whole life choosing to grumble and now there was a danger that she had become, "just a grumble". As I read about her I thought, "Wouldn't it be great if we could all be so blessed that we end up becoming 'just a blessing'!"

The order is important. We are not called by God primarily for marriage, teaching, evangelism, pastoring, administration etc. We are called first to God for God. Then out of this wonderful place of love, blessing, and intimacy we begin to hear God's heartbeat. Then the calling to "go" will come from His passionate concern and not from our good ideas. When we get it the wrong way round we can so easily become a driven people instead of a led people. Before we are called to "do" we are called to "be". Jesus made it clear in John's gospel that we must first "abide" which leads on to fruit bearing.[12]

Brian McClaren presses this point home in his book, *The Story We Find Ourselves In*.[13] His lead character, Neo, had been a pastor, but leaves that to become a teacher and then his father dies and he has to move back home to look after his senile mother. He writes, "It was all the same. Different jobs, different titles, different cities, but the same calling to enjoy God's blessing so that I could be a blessing to others, whether to a church, to a classroom or to my mother."

So the order is important, but it is also important that our primary call is followed by our secondary one – to go. There is no doubt that the call of God on our lives is a "many splendoured thing". How, then do we discern what God has called each of us to? When I first came to know Christ I knew that my life had a purpose to it, but that purpose was only revealed gradually.

Endnotes:

1. Storms, Sam, The Singing God, Creation House, 1998.
2. Genesis 1:31
3. Zephaniah 1:18
4. John 3:16
5. Luke 19:41
6. Mark 11:12
7. Jeremiah 3:19
8. Zephaniah 3:17

9. Guinness, Os, The Call, Authentic Lifestyle, 2001.

10. Genesis 12:2

11. Lewis, C.S., The Great Divorce, HarperCollins, 2002.

12. John 15

13. McLaren, Brian D., The Story We Find Ourselves In, Jossey Bass, 2008.

5
The Call of God

After only a few weeks of committing my life to Christ I was asked to give my testimony at a small meeting. For the first time I spoke about my faith publicly. I think my little talk lasted no more than a few minutes and at the end I sat down feeling exposed and vulnerable, vowing never to put myself through such a thing again. After the meeting had finished an elderly lady came up to speak to me. She said nothing about my testimony. Instead she looked me in the eye and said, "You are going to be a missionary." I was shocked! Firstly, I had never heard of such things as "prophecy" or a "word of knowledge" and had no idea what would have led her to say such a thing. But secondly, into my mind came something that had happened to me when I was about fourteen.

It was at the time when our form at school was being prepared for confirmation. I had gone forward with the rest of my friends, though I knew little about the faith I was supposed to be confirming. But half way through the course I committed some misdemeanour – which was not unusual. I was called in to the Headmistress's study to which I was no stranger. She suggested that I wasn't ready to be confirmed and that she was thinking of withdrawing my name from the list. I can't remember why, but my best friend had accompanied me and she immediately spoke up for me and assured the headmistress that I would in future behave myself and that she would see to it, or something to that effect.

Then the Headmistress turned to me and asked, in a resigned tone of voice, "Whatever do you think you are going to do with your life?" To my amazement, and certainly to hers, I said, "I am going to be a missionary."

To this day I have no idea what made me say such a thing. I had never met a missionary, never even read about missionary work. But four years later, when the old lady said those words to me, that is what came flooding back into my mind. Was this to be God's purpose for my life, I wondered?

A few years later David and I, with our tiny first baby, left Liverpool Docks on a drizzly, grey day in October for a five week voyage to Chile. We had both felt we needed at least to try the door to the mission field and this one had flown open – I admit, slightly to our dismay. Little did we know, as we stood on the deck, watching the land slowly disappearing into the distance, that we were embarking on the adventure of a lifetime that would change us forever.

God's ways, fifty years later, still amaze me! Back then my thinking was that everyone who wanted to be really committed to God's service would end up in "full time" service. I still believe that, but now I would define "full time" rather differently. I once differentiated between the "spiritual" and the "secular", and would have elevated one above another. It was very liberating to realise that my time in the tax office had been as much a calling and as spiritual as my time in Chile. Once we call Jesus "Lord" our lives, by definition, are lived to do His will and promote His kingdom everywhere we go and whatever we do.

As Oz Guinness writes, "Calling is the truth that God calls us to Himself so decisively that everything we are, everything we do, and everything we have is invested with a special devotion, dynamism and direction lived out as a response to His summons and service."[1]

It would have helped during those first ten years in Chile if I had known that liberating truth. After hours of feeding babies, changing nappies, cooking meals, washing endless dirty clothes (no washing machines!) and struggling with the children's Spanish homework, I not only felt as if I was in a spiritual desert, but I had completely lost any sense of "calling". I knew that because I was a Christian my life still had meaning to it, but the purpose had got buried beneath the business of bringing up four children in rather difficult conditions.

I now know that differentiating between full time service and secular work is a big mistake. It seems to me that we all have three distinct calls on our lives.

The first is the primary one: to God – to love Him with all our hearts, soul, strength and mind. Then comes the secondary one: to love our neighbour as ourselves. The first two apply to everyone, they are God's general call to each one of us. It's the call to be salt and light, to be a blessing, to be a witness, to be an ambassador of the kingdom and to be able to give a reason for the hope that is within us. The third call is the specific one which differs for each of us according to our situation, talents, personality and experiences.

These specific callings may change with the changing seasons of life. So for the first ten years in Chile I was first and foremost a wife and mother. I had little energy for more than that. I eventually ran a women's Bible Study group in our home, but only with the help of an older woman, without whom I could never have done it. The church planting that David was involved with never had first call on my time. Our marriage, our home and our children had. It was what the situation called for at the time, though probably not what I am particularly gifted at.

But God graciously gave me the ability to fulfil the task. Hospitality also became a great part of my life. David headed up the mission in our region and later in all three countries of Chile, Bolivia and Peru. We would meet missionaries arriving in the port and they would stay with us for a week or so before they were deployed to their stations.

Because we lived near the sea many of the missionaries from other regions came for their summer holidays with us, and as our own team grew so we became the hub for all the single missionaries who loved to spend time with a family. It wasn't all hard work, because we gained as much from our "aunties" as they gained from us. They were the only family our girls knew and we are forever grateful for their input. Hospitality is not a special gift of mine, but at that time I think God gave me what was needed to cope with it.

Looking back now, I can see how God was at work in my life during those years of what seemed at the time a spiritual desert. I felt as if I would never be able to pray again without a toddler crawling over me or pulling at my sleeve. We seemed to stumble from one crisis to the next and gradually I came to the end of my own resources – and God allowed it to happen! But more of that later.

Once the children were all at school and the many health issues seemed to be sorting themselves out, I felt as if I was emerging from a very dark tunnel where I had been trapped. With the freedom to look around I began visiting some of the churches that had been planted in our region and gradually began to draw some of the women together to teach them skills in leading a Bible study group.

Though I hadn't a lot of experience I knew how important it was for them to know the Bible and at the time we had a missionary living with us who had belonged to the Navigators – a great organisation that helped new Christians learn their Bible. Our missionary friend, Chris Simons, taught me the Navigator method of Bible study which I found so easy to pass on. It had three parts to it:

First was *Discovery*, where the aim was to uncover the background to the passage they were studying. So if it was the letter to the Ephesians, then we needed to know who wrote it, where was it written, at what time and who the recipients might be.

The next part was *Understanding*, where the group would try to get to the reason it was written and what the passage was trying to convey.

Lastly was the *Application*, which was the best part, when the question asked was: "How does this apply to our lives today?" It was such a simple format to pass on.

I loved the time I spent with the women in those churches. I began also to do some speaking and found I enjoyed it – not just the preparation, but also the actual speaking. It felt natural and though my Spanish was not always grammatically correct, I was fluent enough to make myself understood (though as always, in another culture one can make some bad mistakes!)

Around this time I took a long weekend off, leaving David to cope with the children. My great friend, Anderly Hardy, and I took a bus to the South of Chile (about 400 miles) to visit a missionary friend who worked amongst the Mapuche Indians. It was a long journey, but it felt so amazing for the first time in years to have a break away from the family. On the Sunday we accompanied our friend to visit one of the little Indian reductions and attend their church service.

We were both asked to say a few words of greeting, which was a normal request. But then I was asked to give a word of encouragement to the brethren. I was totally unprepared and could only think of the passage I had been reading that morning which I had found particularly inspiring. It was from 1 Peter and spoke about our inheritance that can never spoil or fade. I found myself getting quite stirred up as I encouraged the little church to "take up their inheritance". *"Hay que tomar su herencia,"* I kept repeating. Little did I know that at that time the Indians were quite militant about reclaiming the land that had been taken from them over the years by the "foreign" farmers and were beginning to demand their "inheritance" back. My friends have never let me forget my meddling in political affairs!

When we eventually returned to England, after seventeen years in Chile, I began again to lead a Bible study and felt it was where my gifting lay. The other things I became involved with were various committees set up to choose missionaries for South America and look after their welfare once there. I felt my experience had fitted me for this task.

The only problem was that I seemed to be the token woman on the committees and I felt my voice was rarely listened to. On several occasions I would query someone's suitability for life in South America, only to discover that they were sent anyway, but would end up back home after a year with the nervous breakdown, as I had predicted.

We had met John and Carol Wimber in 1981. John was the founder of the new Vineyard movement in California and we became good friends. They invited us to stay with them – something that was repeated every summer for the next ten years.

It was in about 1982, while staying in their house, that I had a very strange dream. I dreamt I was wearing a mauve dress and it was drizzling with rain. The rain was wetting my clothes and the dye in the dress was beginning to stain my skin mauve. I awoke with the words, "It's killing me," on my lips. I felt so shaken by the dream that I went into the kitchen where Carol was putting on the coffee and told her. She immediately said that she thought that when I got home I should look at everything I was doing and see what might be "killing me" – emotionally, spiritually or even physically.

This led me to resign from just about everything I was doing. I handed the Bible study over, I came off the committees, and I prepared myself to do nothing but wait. Of course, the usual life of the Vicarage continued. Almost daily I found myself giving tea or coffee to one troubled person after another. Our youngest daughter was still at school and was coming home every day to some crying soul in the kitchen taking up her mother's time. She began to complain and I began to think I had to organise my time a little better.

During our time in Chile I had been introduced to Ruth Carter Stapleton and Francis MacNutt. They had run a course on "Inner Healing" for the Catholics which I and a friend had attended. I had been fascinated by the whole concept of Jesus being able to walk back through time and heal the painful memories that lurked there. So out of interest I attended a counselling course directed by the late Selwyn Hughes. Around the same time John Wimber was conducting a series of meetings in London, which

David and I attended. One afternoon meeting John announced
that during the evening meeting he was going to pray especially
for the pastors, evangelists, teachers, church planters, etc, and as
he went through the list my heart began to sink. I knew I wasn't
a pastor, nor an evangelist, nor any of the others he mentioned.
But then John hesitated for a moment and added, "... and the 'Fish
Cleaners' too." My heart leapt. "That's me!" I thought. I am not
good at fishing, but I don't mind the mess of cleaning the fish after
they have been caught.

So that night I waited anxiously while he called the various
ministries forward. I thought for one awful moment that he had
forgotten the "fish cleaners", but once again, almost as an afterthought, he called them forward. I have no idea if anyone else but
me went forward for that particular calling. I pushed my way out
of the pew, knocking most of the books off the shelf as I went in
my anxiety to get to the front. I remember falling on my knees,
sobbing my heart out, and someone coming to pray over me. But
it was the call of God and I shall never forget it.

From that time on I began to think about setting up a prayer/
counselling group in our church in Chorleywood. We eventually
called it, "Pastoral Prayer Ministry" in order to avoid the word
"counselling". We didn't want to be forced into using only qualified
people who would have to obtain some certificate before they
could be involved. About four of us did eventually become
certified with the Association of Christian Counsellors, which
gave the rest of those involved a good covering. David was busy
training a prayer ministry team ready to minister whenever we
had a meeting in the church, expecting that God would confirm
the Word with signs following.[2]

Out of the 250 people that were eventually authorised to minister
we set aside about 25 people who were mature Christians to spend

time with people who needed a little more attention than could be given after a Sunday service. The Bedwells had by this time come on to the staff of the church and Richard was invaluable in overseeing this ministry. He had a natural feel for counselling and both he and his wife Prue have given the last thirty years to it, day in and day out. Prue and I did most of the teaching, as well as seeing people together every Friday from early morning until the evening.

In 1996 David retired from St Andrew's and I was no longer able to minister in that church. It was a wrench for me in particular to say goodbye to a ministry that God had so plainly laid on my heart. But one of the criteria of this ministry was that we only prayed with people who were members of our church. I felt that we would be inundated if we opened it up further. In any case, surely each church should be responsible for the health and maturity of its own members? I still did some travelling and teaching on the subject, helping others to set up a similar ministry in their churches, but gradually I realised that that time in my life was over. The Call of God had moved on. And He was beginning to use me more beyond the local church.

God uses us in particular ways according to our situation, experience and talents. It behoves us all to listen to God's voice for what is on His Agenda for us as individuals during this moment in time.

As I have pondered this I have begun to realise in what a variety of ways I have been blessed by the help of other people. The general call on them is to be a blessing, but the specific manner of that blessing is totally different for each of them. One of my friends is a little wealthier than I am and her generosity has blessed me over and over. Another friend is particularly gifted at hospitality and so often, at just the right moment, an invitation has come to spend the evening with them. Yet another person is an extremely good driver and navigator and time and again has taken me to a meeting, got me there on time, and supported me whilst there. God provides each of us with specific talents and it is up to us to use them to bless those around us.

Endnotes:

1. Guinness, Oz, The Call, Authentic Lifestyle, 2001.
2. 1 Thessalonians 1:5

6
Commitment

When we left Liverpool Docks on that drizzly October day and set sail for South America, had I been asked I would have said that I was totally committed to God and to doing His will. After all, I had been to Bible College, had even preached in the open air, and now we were giving up our home and family for the mission field. Surely that said it all. But self-knowledge only comes with time and testing, as I was soon to find out.

In the latter years in Chile we used to spend some of our spare time panning for gold in a nearby river. It was great fun and there was always the chance we might find a nugget. At first we were deceived by finding what looked like gold, but was in fact "fool's gold". It looks the same, but there are differences. Fool's gold crumbles under pressure and doesn't shine in the dark. The real thing is tough, resilient and bright in all conditions. Similarly, I was soon to know what was real in my commitment and what was just imagined.

King Solomon writes of gold being tested by fire.[1] God will turn up the heat sometimes to test us and reveal the dross in our lives. And I was soon to experience the discomfort of God's purifying work in my life. At the time I was miserable and couldn't understand what was happening to me and why. Only with hindsight have I been able to see the way that God used the difficulties of those early years in Chile.

The testing started in the first week. We arrived in the port of Valparaiso after five weeks at sea, then took a train to Santiago, the capital, and from there took the night train down south to the mission centre in Temuco.

We left Santiago in sweltering heat and not wanting the baby to get overheated, we left her uncovered for the night. No one had told us how cold the nights were and that there was also quite a marked difference in temperature between the north and the south of the country. Charlotte must have picked up a chill during the night and a few days after arrival in Temuco she developed pneumonia. It was a frightening start for us.

After a few months it was time to move ourselves and our luggage to a little one-horse town called Chol Chol which became a slightly more permanent home. It was situated about two hours from Temuco. Most of the way was a dirt track and during the summer the dust seemed to seep into every crevice. During the winter it was often impassable with flood waters or mud and so we had to go the long way round by a little town called Nueva Imperial.

The day we were due to make the move David was unwell, so he travelled in the front cabin of the van with Charlotte and the driver, while I sat on top of the luggage in the open air at the back of the Unimog – a strange vehicle, ideal for rough roads, but clearly comfort was far from the maker's mind. It was high off the ground and once our luggage was packed into the back, I was left perched precariously on the top. I clung on to whatever I could find and bounced like a ping pong ball for two miserable hours with the dust swirling around me, blinding my eyes, clogging my nostrils and permeating my clothes.

I admit that I cried most of the way! In our preparation for the mission field we had read a little book entitled, *Have We No Rights?* Sitting up in bed in our comfortable semi in Wallington reading that book, I had bravely thought that I really was ready for anything. But it is one thing to imagine oneself enduring hardships and quite another when one actually meets them. I found I was nowhere near as ready as I had thought to suffer for the sake of the gospel. My image of myself was beginning to crumble.

Four months after this ghastly journey we had to make another one, this time by bus, which was full of the local Mapuche Indians with their wares to sell in Temuco. We needed to see a doctor for David's mouth infection, so we stayed at the mission house there for a few days.

Suddenly on the Saturday morning of 21st May, 1960 we were woken early with the house rocking from side to side. To our horror we watched the baby's cot slide across the floor towards the window. We had no idea what was happening so we leapt out of bed, grabbed the baby and tore down the stairs, by which time all was quiet again so we climbed back up the stairs feeling a little sheepish and stupid. No one else in the house had appeared.

The next afternoon we were out for a walk in the local plaza when the south of Chile was hit by the biggest earthquake ever recorded. It lasted for five minutes and was the most terrifying experience I can ever remember. We hung on to a tree, clutching each other and the baby, while all around us people were screaming and crying out to the Virgin Mary for help. Terrified passengers were staring out their car windows as they bounced this way and that, their drivers at a loss to know what to do. All around the façades of the houses were crashing to the ground. Crowds streamed out of the local cinema looking around them in disbelief. I thought the world was coming to an end.

Details about that earthquake can be read in Wikipedia: "The 1960 Valdivia earthquake or Great Chilean earthquake of 22 May 1960 is, to date, the most powerful earthquake ever recorded, rating 9.5 on the moment magnitude scale. It occurred in the afternoon (19:11 GMT, 14:11 local time) and its resulting tsunami affected southern Chile, Hawaii, Japan, the Philippines, eastern New Zealand, southeast Australia, and the Aleutian Islands in Alaska."

The coast line was said to have sunk five to seven feet for several hundred miles to the south of Concepcion. The sea came in and never went back leaving a line of hills as islands.

A few days later we took the infamous Unimog and returned to Chol Chol. The wide, fast flowing Chol Chol river had to be crossed by a high, long, wooden bridge in order to reach the village. We had no idea how it had fared during the quake.

On sight it looked shaky but still standing, so David sent me across on foot, carrying the baby and he tentatively drove the van, with the door open ready to jump at the first sign of the bridge collapsing. In fact, it was closed soon after for major repairs. But then began a period of many disturbed nights.

In company with our fellow missionaries we slept fully dressed in one of the school rooms downstairs, ready to race to the door the moment the house began to shake, which it did for many months.

At that point we had been in Chile only six months and all I wanted to do was to go back to England to solid ground and safety. All David would say was that if God wanted us dead we could die as easily crossing the road in England! It didn't comfort me very much.

One other journey from those years stands out in my memory and that is one we had to make on the back of an onion lorry. It was in the middle of winter, which in the south is wet and very muddy. We had made one of our occasional visits into town just for the day. We left Temuco in the late afternoon on the bus, just as it was getting dark. But the bus broke down half way and we were left stranded at the side of the road with all the other passengers. Vehicles to Chol Chol were few and far between, but to our relief a lorry came into sight and offered us all a lift. We clambered up the side with our baby and sat ourselves on top of a cargo of onions. The onion mountain on the lorry was soon blanketed by passengers all perched precariously on top. David held the baby, I clung to him and we both hung on to the long, very English looking umbrella which we had with us and that David had stuck right down into the onions to give us some stability. We eventually arrived home, wet and cold, but in one piece.

There was further testing to come. This had been but the beginning of a long process, which was eventually bringing me to the place God had wanted me in all along and that was crying out to Him for help. As I have thought about the issue of commitment I have realised that it can include all the aspects I have mentioned and many more excellent ingredients – but without a deep knowledge of one's inadequacy and weakness, the sort of commitment that God longs for will still be missing.

The story of King Solomon's great grandson, Asa, is a good illustration of what God is looking for. Asa started his reign as King of Judah really well. He did what was right in the eyes of the Lord and removed the idols which had increased in great number under his grandfather, King Rehoboam. Then, when the Cushites invaded Judah, Asa cried out to God with these great words:

"Lord, there is no one like you to help the powerless against the mighty. Help us, O Lord our God, for we rely on you, and in your name we have come against this vast army. O Lord you are our God, do not let man prevail against you."[2]

And as a result of Asa's prayer the Lord struck down the Cushites.

Then Asa receives a prophesy from Azariah the son of Oded. *"The Lord is with you when you are with him. If you seek him he will be found by you, but if you forsake him, he will forsake you."*[3] It was a warning that Asa should have heeded.

But it is easy to grow slack when everything is peaceful and quiet. Asa, the King of Judah, had 25 years of peace and then he was threatened by Baasha, the King of Israel. When confronted by an enemy invasion he did what he thought would get him out of difficulty – he took the silver and gold out of the treasuries of the Lord's temple and his own palace and sent them down to Ben-Hadad, King of Aram, who ruled in Damascus.[4] It seemed to be a good idea and one that did, in fact, work perfectly. The treasure bought Ben-Hadad's help and Baasha was overcome.

But then it was the turn of Hanani the seer to come with a word from God for Asa: *"Because you relied on the King of Aram and not on the Lord your God the army of the King of Aram has escaped from your hand. Were not the Cushites and Libyans a mighty army with great numbers of chariots and horsemen? Yet when you relied on the Lord He delivered them into your hands. **For the eyes of the Lord range throughout the earth to strengthen those whose hearts are fully committed to Him.** You have done a foolish thing and from now on you will be at war."*[5] Soon after this Asa fell sick, but even then he didn't call out to God. Somewhere along the line Asa had compromised his commitment to the Lord.

God loves commitment and actually looks for it. His eyes are searching up and down the villages, towns and cities of our world for hearts that are fully committed to Him. This story caused me to look more carefully at what commitment might really look like.

Asa had a problem and he did what, for many of us, is the most obvious and natural thing to do. He looked for a way through his problems and he thought he had a good idea for resolving them. Isn't that just what we all tend to do? But it was Asa's "good idea" which displeased God. Why? Because though it seemed a good idea, it was not God's idea. God had had no part in it. God had not been Asa's primary resource. Full commitment means that first of all we make God our primary port of call for all our problems. That doesn't mean that we never go to see a doctor or ask others for help, but it does mean that before any of those options we consult God.

For most of us this does not come naturally. As a result of the fall we all have a tendency towards independence. We have a "fall back" mentality. It infiltrates our whole lives. My store cupboard is full of tins of food. My freezer is full of food, ready for any unexpected visitor. I constantly think ahead to plan journeys, preparing myself for every eventuality. And there is nothing wrong with this sort of thinking, except when it infiltrates my whole life and soon becomes my automatic response to every situation – so that whenever there is a problem of any sort I immediately think of a good idea to resolve it. The ideas will come out of a store cupboard of past experiences, the latest book, my training, my friends, or my family. Independence is something we will all struggle with for the rest of our lives. Even if last week, or even yesterday, I remembered to make God my primary resource, today I will have to remind myself to do it again.

It is a little like having two pairs of glasses. The first is an old pair which are safe and comfortable and give me an independent view of everything. The second pair are *kingdom glasses* and they are uncomfortable because they show me the true state of affairs. They show me the truth about my weakness, my poverty and my desperate need of God.

So commitment means that we make God our primary resource, for the simple reason that we have at last recognised our desperate need – that without Him we can do nothing[6] and that we are limited, fallible human beings. Full commitment starts here, but then it grows and begins to be a stubborn persistence to pursue Him and His blessing at all costs. As Azariah counselled Asa after his battle with the Cushites, *"The Lord is with you when you are with Him and if you seek Him he will be found by you."* If we seek Him! But it all starts with desperation and then a conviction that God has what we need.

Once God sees the beginnings of commitment He strengthens it. As I have grown in the Christian life, I have discovered that there's an ebb and flow to God's dealings with me. Sometimes God seems to be hiding Himself. At other times He seems more obviously present. It seems He is toning up my spiritual muscles and trying to mature me. It also creates hunger within me. When we haven't felt His touch for a while we begin to seek Him more earnestly. *"You will seek me and find me when you seek me with all your heart. I will be found by you."*[7] Hunger is a great catalyst for seeking God.

The evangelist, Kathryn Kuhlman, had an amazing ministry in America during the 1940's and 50s. But there was a time in her life when she took a wrong turn and was out of the ministry for about six years. Towards the end of this time she was out walking and saw a sign in the road which read "DEAD END". When she saw those words she said that she felt a heartache so great that it could not be put into words. She had lost the wonderful filling of the

Holy Spirit. She had lost all the power she had previously known. At that point she stopped in the road and prayed, "Dear Jesus, I surrender all, I give it all to you. Take my body, take my heart. All I am is yours."[8] Soon after this she was preaching once again to thousands and amazing miracles were taking place. Hunger and desperation for God is a prerequisite for knowing His blessing.

But I wasn't yet desperate enough. The coping façade was still there. Sometimes there has to be a breaking down before there can be a building up and there was more tearing down of the "image" still to be done.

Endnotes:

1. Proverbs 17:3
2. 2 Chronicles 14:11
3. 2 Chronicles 15:2
4. 2 Chronicles 16:1
5. 2 Chronicles 16:7
6. John 15:5
7. Jeremiah 29:13
8. Buckingham, Jamie, Daughter of Destiny, Bridge-Logos, 1999.

7
Anointing

After a couple of years working in Chol Chol among the Mapuche Indians we were sent to the port of Valparaiso to plant churches in an urban situation. For the first seven years in Valparaiso we lived in an old church hall. The English ex-pats who had lived and worked in Valparaiso had had their homes on Cerro Alegre – "Happy Hill". They had built a church there with a large hall behind it. Gradually, as Valparaiso became more crowded, they had moved to the nearby more salubrious resort of Vina Del Mar. So for fifty years the church and hall had stood empty and had hardly been used. It seemed to offer the ideal location for starting a work there. And since the hall had electricity, gas, running water and a toilet, David felt sure that we could use it as living accommodation. We moved up there from Chol Chol in 1962.

I shall never forget that bus journey up from the South. Charlotte was three and Debby was a baby of a few weeks and she cried non-stop all the way. We arrived in Valparaiso one hot afternoon completely exhausted. We walked into the hall and I sat on top of a pile of very dusty old carpets to feed the baby while Charlotte ran around getting grey with the dust and dirt of fifty years! I sat there with tears running down my face.

"How can I possibly bring up two children in this hell hole?" I asked myself.

But David was as cheerful as ever. There were beds stacked in the hall, left over from some missionaries who had gone home a few months earlier. David made up the beds and we lit a little paraffin stove and cooked up some sort of meal, then we boiled a kettle and tried to wash the children down before tucking them into bed. It was a difficult start.

But we struggled on and gradually the place took shape. David built rooms on the stage at one end. He shut off a corridor and made it into a long narrow sitting room and then he plumbed in some piping for a bathroom and put in hot water. With a gas stove working and hot water in the taps I began to feel I could cope at last.

We lived in that hall for seven years. Becky was born in Valparaiso and our last baby, Tasha, in England when we had leave in 1965. She came back to the church hall aged four months. So our four daughters spent their childhood on Cerro Alegre. The roof leaked when it rained and the dust was always a problem when the strong winds blew up every afternoon. There was only one window we could see out of, so the inside was always gloomy. Our girls went from one health crisis to another. One developed a primary complex of TB, another nearly died from peritonitis, they all had Scarlet Fever, and I had a month confined to bed with Hepatitis.

By the end of seven years I was worn out physically, but more seriously, emotionally. I had begun to have what I now know were panic attacks. It was frightening and made me feel out of control and I began to feel as if I was letting David down by not being strong and ready for anything. I kept remembering the missionary books I had read and the amazing sacrifices they had made in Africa and China; the terrible living conditions and how they had even packed their belongings in a coffin because they knew that was very probably the only way they would be going home.

I was mortified by my weakness and refused to let David tell any of the other missionaries or ask for help. One fateful afternoon we had been out to tea with one of our church members. I had spent most of the time in the bathroom, pretending that one of the children had needed the toilet when in reality I was continually sponging my face down to try and control the feelings of panic which kept overwhelming me. On the way home I sobbed with desperation and arrived home tear-stained and drained.

As I entered the house I was greeted by one of the missionary nurses. We had always maintained an open home policy for the other missionaries, so they all knew where the key was kept and would let themselves into the house, whether we were there or not, usually putting the kettle on and waiting for us to get back.

So there was Jean. When she saw me she demanded an explanation of what was wrong. Out came the whole sorry story. Bless her heart, she immediately took control and insisted that we visit a doctor and then asked us when we had last had a break. In fact, we had not had a holiday for six years, except for our leave in the UK. Somehow, the thought had not crossed our minds. I think we thought that we lived near the sea and that was somehow sufficient. In any case, money was limited and David has never been a great one for holidays. He says he is always relaxed and doesn't need to go away to be any more relaxed.

When Jean heard this she immediately said she was going to arrange for us to go away for a summer break and she would come with us to help with the children. It was such a relief to have someone take over and with the help of some little pills the doctor gave me I began to improve.

We had our break in the south of Chile camping by one of the lakes. Jean came and Clorinda, a little Mapuche girl, came to help with the cooking over a camp fire. It was a great success and became the first of yearly camping trips to one of Chile's many beauty spots. A few years later we left for our second leave in England. By the time we had been in England for nearly a year, with David doing deputation work, I was physically well and to my relief the panic attacks had abated. But I knew that I was still spiritually at a very low ebb. I knew too that we would be returning to some very difficult situations in the Diocese and to some political unrest in the country. How would I cope?

We left Southampton on a boat heading for Buenos Aires. I remember climbing the gangway and praying as I went: "Oh God, I can't get off this boat the way I am getting on. You will have to do something." We were travelling with a new missionary, Jenny Thornton, and she and I spent our time on the deck chatting and getting to know one another. She had obviously had some Pentecostal-type experience that had changed her life and I was curious. I kept questioning her and eventually I asked her outright what difference this experience had made to her.

She paused and then answered, "I fell in love with Jesus."

I felt as if someone had kicked me in the stomach. I knew that was what I needed. So I began to pray. Every night after the children were in bed I would leave David in charge and make my way to the back of the boat where I could be quite alone.

I would gaze at the stars and cry out to God, "Please, please, God do something. I need something, anything." But usually after that prayer I would add, very quietly, "But I don't want to get all emotional, nor do I want to speak in tongues." Night after night I kept up my vigil. But nothing happened.

I was getting desperate.

We were nearing Buenos Aires and then there would be a short flight over the Andes and we would be back in it the middle of it all once again. So I began to alter my praying. I began by confessing every sin I could remember and as I did so, I realised that I had never really made a true confession. I had always prefaced my confession with the little word "if": "*If* I sinned when I did/said... then I repent."

Now I prayed, "Lord, when I said/did this I sinned, please forgive me." Then I told the Lord that if I cried it was okay and if I got emotional, well okay to that too. I knew that I had finished with trying to box God in. One night soon after this, clambering into my bunk, I remembered the verse, *"And Joy cometh in the morning."*[1] The next day I went to read my Bible and it fell open at Luke 11:9:

"Ask and it will be given to you; seek and you will find; knock and the door will be opened to you. For everyone who asks receives; he who seeks finds; and to him who knocks the door will be opened."

I pondered the verse. I had been asking for nearly three weeks. Could it be that somewhere along the line I had received, but just wasn't the sort of person for something ground shaking to happen to? Perhaps I just had to accept that God had heard my prayer and act as if He had? So with that thought in mind I went up on deck.

I said to myself, "What would I do if I really had received the Holy Spirit?" And in answer: "I would tell someone," I thought. Jenny was already on deck, so I just stood beside her and told her that I had been filled with the Spirit. Almost before I had finished saying those words something inside me began to explode. I filled up as if I was a balloon and thought that I might just float off the ship and into the Atlantic at any minute.

The sensation of fullness was overwhelming, but glorious.

The change was immediate. The world looked different. Everything was in Technicolor. God's creation seemed to have come alive. But best of all was the longing for the Word of God. I devoured it. I think it was the fact that I began wearing out Bibles that convinced David that this was something very good and, after about three months of living with a "new" wife, he asked me to lay hands on him and pray for him. So began a new episode in our lives. We were now card carrying Charismatics!

That long preamble was to underline the amazing fact that there is still more of the Holy Spirit's anointing available to us than anything we have yet experienced. Of course, we have the Spirit when we come to Christ. But there is always more. Paul instructs the Ephesians to *"go on being filled with the Spirit."*[2] What I experienced on the boat was not just a one off. A few weeks later the Spirit of God overwhelmed me once again and this time I spoke in tongues. There have been so many instances when God has met me in a special way with a further anointing.

However, I think there are certain conditions for experiencing the "more" that God has for us. The most important is hunger and thirst. There has to be a felt need and I had certainly experienced that! The Holy Spirit is given to be our Helper, Comforter, Guide and Strengthener. He is the power source for ministry. We just can't do without Him. The best place to be is at the end of our own resources when we know without a shadow of a doubt, *"that without Him we can do nothing."*[3]

A.W. Tozer, the American author and pastor, speaking about the Holy Spirit, said that before we can be filled with the Spirit, the desire to be filled must be all-consuming. It must be for the time, the biggest thing in our life – so acute, so intrusive as to crowd out everything else. The degree of fullness in my life accords perfectly with the intensity of my true desire. We have as much of God as we actually want. In Psalm 107 we read that God fills the hungry with good things, not the satisfied. And in Jeremiah we read, *"And you will seek me and find me, when you search for me with all your heart."*[4]

So the first condition is *hunger* and the next follows on: *openness*. On the boat I had been giving God conditions for the way I wanted Him to answer my prayer. I had overlooked the fact that God is God – the Creator of the Universe. I was calling Him Lord and then telling Him what to do. So often we box Him in to our ideas of how He should work, both in our lives and in our churches. In the end we settle for a small God that we can control.

When the Toronto Blessing first broke out in the Airport Christian Fellowship, David went to see what was happening, but also to be refreshed himself. In one meeting he was trying to receive from God when a man at the back of the hall kept calling out, "Big God!" Over and over, at the top of his voice, he kept repeating himself. David felt quite annoyed and hoped someone would tell him to be quiet. But the noise continued until David began to realise that it was God trying to catch his attention:

"David, I'm a Big God."

Sometimes God has to shock us out of our complacency.

Then we should make sure that we have cleared the decks and that there is nothing left to prevent us receiving whatever God has for us. On the boat I spent time examining my life and confessing whatever the Holy Spirit brought into my mind. But once that has been done, with confidence we can ask God to bless us. It may feel selfish to be asking for ourselves, but we have nothing to bless others with unless we are first blessed ourselves. So to call out for more of God's blessing, anointing and gifting for ourselves is a must.

When Jacob fought with the "man" in the night before he was to meet Esau, he realised he was really struggling with God. Then he said to the Lord, *"I will not let you go unless you bless me."*[5] Jabez, in the book of Chronicles, is only remembered for his selfish prayer to God – a prayer that God answered: *"Oh, that you would bless **me** and enlarge **my** territory,"*[6] he prayed. Charismatics are often accused of wanting just another bless-up. But how can we spill over in blessing to others if we are not brimful ourselves?

And we have to give God time. In our instant world of mobile phones and email we are not good at waiting. Patience is a virtue, but also it is a time of testing and growth. God loves commitment. *"His eyes range throughout the earth to strengthen those whose hearts are fully committed to Him."*[7]

One of the tests of commitment is whether or not we are prepared to wait for God to answer our prayers. If God were to wave a magic wand and give us whatever we asked for, whenever we asked for it, how mature would we be? Wouldn't that be to keep us being like babies who, when they cry, are instantly picked up and fed? Part of our journey to maturity is to learn to trust God and hang in there even when we don't know exactly what He is doing and the heavens seem like brass.

I remember hearing the testimony of a young girl who had had anorexia very badly. By the time she was eighteen she had been in and out of hospital many times and on this last occasion the doctor had told her, quite honestly, that if she starved her body one more time she would die. She said that she knew he spoke the truth, but felt hopeless. She knew she hadn't the strength to beat the compulsion to starve herself.

When she went home from the hospital she locked herself in her bedroom, lay down on the floor and told God that she wasn't going to move until He touched her life and set her free. She waited all night, but in the morning God visited her and from then on the anorexia lost its power in her life.

So *patience* and then the twin virtue of *persistence* are needed. The story about a friend arriving at midnight and catching his host by surprise with an empty bread-bin was told by Jesus to emphasise our need to go on seeking the Holy Spirit. The host knocks on his neighbour's door until at last the neighbour responds to his demands. Jesus ended the story with the famous words, *"Ask and it will be given to you; seek and you will find; knock and the door will be opened to you. For everyone who asks receives; he who seeks finds, and he who knocks it will be opened to him."*[8]

I am no expert in prayer, but I have experienced enough to know that God does answer prayer – just not always in the ways we might imagine, nor in the timeframe we would desire. Often I have been surprised by His answer and occasionally mystified, especially when it is to do with healing and someone we have prayed for with great longing, to see them healed, has died. The way I have personally handled this is to tell myself again that, *"God is* [still] *good and His love* [still] *endures forever"*[9] and that one day I will see the whole picture and understand. But more on prayer and healing later.

The Holy Spirit not only causes us to "go" for God but empowers us to do the job. The results of my fresh anointing were manifold. First, as I have said, was a hunger and love for God's Word. I just couldn't get enough of it. I was so full up that it naturally began to spill over and, I hope, bless others. I started mentoring other women – mostly my friends at first – then it seemed natural to follow this with some teaching and eventually I began to speak in public on a regular basis.

Looking back it was a joy and privilege to have a platform from which to share all that God was showing me.

God pulls down, but He also builds up. There were many difficulties ahead for us in Chile, not least having to live through a revolution, yet another major earthquake and the heartbreaking decision to send our oldest and then our second daughter to finish their schooling back in England. But despite all this, I found a greater strength than I had previously known. God had changed me and to Him be the glory.

Endnotes:

1. Psalm 30:5
2. Ephesians 5:18
3. John 15:5
4. Jeremiah 29:13-14
5. Genesis 32:22
6. 1 Chronicles 4:9-10
7. 2 Chronicles 16:9
8. Luke 11:5-13
9. 2 Chronicles 5:13

8
Adventure into Healing

As I have already recounted, our first years in Chile were spent in Chol Chol, a small frontier town which served the outlying farms and Indian reductions. The roads were all dirt track and through the summer the dust would seep into every crack and crevice, and in the winter the mud could be knee deep. Possibly due to the dust David contracted an infection which was similar to foot and mouth disease. His mouth broke out into ulcers so big that they made you gasp. His temperature soared and at night his sweat would soak the mattress. He was in so much pain that he could eat nothing but sops and could barely open his mouth to speak.

This went on for months. We went into Temuco to see a doctor, travelling on that rickety old bus, accompanied by the chickens and garden produce inside and the sheep tied onto the roof-rack outside. But he told us that there was no treatment and that nothing they could do would help, but that eventually it would wear itself out. Meanwhile, David was getting weaker and weaker.

After about three months we had come to the conclusion that if he didn't get better in the next few weeks we would have to consider packing up and going home.

The little Anglican Church in Chol Chol had been praying for this poor new "gringo" missionary, but now they decided they must up the level of prayer, so they suggested that David come to the church one evening and they would anoint him with oil and pray over him. Healing was not something we had had much experience of. We had not been taught about it at Bible College, except to be told that the gifts were withdrawn when we received the canon of Scripture and that today God healed through doctors. But we had both read enough missionary biographies to know that God sometimes broke these "rules". So, with very little faith, at least on my part, David submitted to the anointing. He was healed almost immediately! Looking back, that was my first experience of God's power to heal.

When we eventually came into the things of the Spirit we began to explore the whole area of the gifts of the Spirit, of which we had been so ignorant. One of our first introductions to the world of supernatural healing was at an evangelistic campaign held in the Valparaiso Football Stadium. I went along on the first evening with a friend and Gigi Avila, the evangelist from Central America, first preached the gospel and then called for all the deaf people to stand and he prayed for them. We were sitting about half way up the stands and to my amazement a young man began to shout loudly that he had been healed. I admit to wondering if he had been a "plant". But this thought was soon dispersed when he began to leap over the wooden benches to get to the front and I recognised him as a young man from one of our own churches. I knew he was deaf and was in fact booked to have an operation on his ear.

I was so excited that I rushed home to David and told him that all the family should go the next evening, which we did. The stadium was packed with people, so when it came time for the healing ministry to begin and the people surged forward, David gave our four girls strict instructions to stay close to me while he went down to the front to watch what was happening. It was chaotic and at some point I mislaid our third daughter, Becky, and her little friend. But David spied them down at the front watching what was happening. Later, when he ticked them off for being disobedient, they told him that they "just wanted to see a miracle", which after all was why he had gone down there also! But it was a mystery as to how they managed to push through the crowds. He said that the crowd had parted for him because he was wearing a dog collar and they thought he was a Catholic priest. However, the two girls explained that they had just waited for another healing to take place, when the preacher would shout, *"Quien fue?"* (Who did it?) and all the people would raise their arms to cry "Jesus" – at which point the girls skipped through underneath!

It was an exciting time, especially as healings took place that we had never expected to see in all our lives. For example, we heard of numbers of people who were having cavities in their teeth filled. Several were from our own churches, so we had the opportunity to verify these miracles. However, the model of ministry that we encountered in Chile did not sit well with us and so, though we prayed for people, we didn't as yet practice the ministry of healing on a regular basis in our churches.

After seventeen years in Chile we decided it was time to bring the whole family home to finish their education in England. We went to St Andrew's in 1977 and when we arrived there we discovered that the most popular service was a once a month sung Folk Communion, in which those who wanted ministry came up after taking communion and knelt at the rails where they were prayed for with the laying on of hands by the clergy. It was a tidy model, appreciated by everyone, but I don't remember hearing of anyone getting healed.

When John Wimber paid his first visit to our church in 1981 we saw a model exercised by the laity that we could wholeheartedly embrace. After that visit David began a regular healing ministry training programme for our church members. Very soon the news got out and people came from far and wide because they knew we would pray for them. We needed a bigger and bigger team and eventually we had about 250 people authorised to minister after services in the church.

David wrote a book called *Come Holy Spirit* which set out everything he was learning about ministry in the power of the Spirit. It became a bestseller and was used as a basis for developing the training days. Over the years we have seen some amazing healings, but we have still had some major disappointments. With the disappointments came the temptation to give up. Several factors have personally kept us going.

First is the understanding of the kingdom of God that John Wimber brought to us – the kingdom that was the continuing theme in the preaching of Jesus. Derek Morphew's helpful book, *Breakthrough*, written later, deals with the subject the most thoroughly. In it he writes, "The New Testament view of the kingdom can be summarised in four statements: the kingdom will come; the kingdom has come; the kingdom is coming immediately; and the kingdom will be delayed."[1] It's the mystery of the "now and the not yet" of the kingdom. Jesus taught in terms of two ages – the present and the future. He taught about the coming kingdom and the end of the age (Matthew 24 & 25). But He also taught that the kingdom had already come. *"But if I drive out demons by*

the spirit of God, then the kingdom of God has come upon you."[2]
Derek Morphew explains this by repeating an illustration first
used by Oscar Cullmann: "The final 'push' of the Allied invasion
of Europe was called D-Day. As later history has shown, this was
the decisive battle of the Second World War. Once the Allies had
successfully set up a military position within Europe, it was only
a matter of time before Hitler's armies were defeated. However,
D-Day was not the end of the war. It took months before all the
Axis powers were mopped up and Hitler finally surrendered. This
was V-Day, the moment of the final victory. The time in between
D-Day and V-Day was a period of delay when the war was won,
but not yet won."[3] In fact, there were more casualties of war in
between these two dates than in all of the previous years.

This means that in the healing ministry when the sick are healed
in the name of Jesus, it is a sign that the kingdom has come. But
when someone remains sick, even after much prayer, it means
that the kingdom has not yet come in all its fullness. When the
latter happens, "...there will be no more death or mourning or
crying or pain, for the old order of things has passed away."[4] In
the meantime we press on knowing that we will see signs and
wonders whenever the gospel is preached, but they are just signs
– signs of the coming kingdom.

In the book of Hebrews it states that God has put everything
under the feet of Jesus. Satan was overcome, his minions were
vanquished. It was done, signed and sealed on the cross. But the
statement goes on to say that, "...in putting everything under him,
God left nothing that is not subject to him. Yet at present we do
not see everything subject to Him."[5] We live in the overlap of the
kingdom that has come, but has not yet come in its fullness. This
enabled me to understand better the mystery of healing. "Why are
some people not healed? This is because the kingdom has broken

through but has not yet taken over. It is here, but in a provisional sense. The final takeover of the kingdom will occur at the Second Coming. Until then the present world continues."[6]

So with this understanding we were freed to pursue ministry in the power of the Spirit with faith and integrity. I didn't have to deny the reality and pain of those who remained sick, but I could still pray in the hope of seeing a sign of the kingdom in someone's life who might be miraculously healed. There are still some faith groups who feel that to emphasise this teaching is to diminish faith, so they insist on a "positive confession" which means nothing negative must be mentioned. In fact, the wonderful song of Matt Redman's, *Blessed be your Name*, which contains the words, "On the road marked with suffering, though there is pain in the offering, blessed be Your Name" would not be popular in such churches. This may be helpful to some, but for us it felt as if we were denying the reality of what we experienced. And, pastorally, I felt concerned for those who were not healed. By implication they could so easily feel that it was their fault they were still sick, because they had not had enough faith.

Something else which has always bothered me about going forward for prayer, especially when I am definitely not feeling a 100% myself, is that people will pray over me and feel that they can't stop until something happens, which is both tiring and embarrassing. Two years ago I was in Ireland at a New Wine Conference. My back, which has never been my strong point, was very painful, so in desperation I went forward for prayer. An elderly coupled prayed for me. The wife laid her hands on my back, invited the Holy Spirit to come and then told the back to be healed in Jesus' name. That was it! It was such a relief. I sat down not feeling much better, but by the end of the evening my back was pain free.

Long prayers do not mean more power! In fact, if we used Jesus as our role model we would never pray those long, waffling prayers ever again. He was brief and to the point. He said, *"Be clean"* to a man with leprosy[7]; *"Young man I say to you get up"*[8] to the widow of Nain's dead son. He told the storm, *"Be quiet, be still."*[9] And so it goes on – short orders to the kingdom of darkness. It was these two aspects of the healing ministry – the "now and the not yet'" of the kingdom and the sort of prayers Jesus prayed – that first gave me confidence to obey the command Jesus gave the twelve and then the seventy-two to *"heal the sick."*[10]

Quite early on another guideline that David taught the team, and one that I am ever mindful of, was the dignity of the individual. I was made aware of the importance of this at the first London Conference John Wimber ever led in Westminster Central Hall. It was the end of an exciting and busy morning and I was picking up my things to go to lunch. The hall was almost empty except for a small knot of people in one corner. On my way out I wandered over to see what was happening. I was surprised to see five men around a young woman who was lying on the floor with her skirt far too high. The men were commanding the demons to come out of her and she was crying out and writhing in apparent agony. I agreed that she looked, to all intents and purposes, demonized. But my first thought was "propriety". I was disturbed by the young woman's predicament and this gave me more courage than normal.

I asked if I could talk to the young woman. Rather reluctantly, I thought, the men agreed. I bent down and asked her quietly if she was all right. She shook her head and looked at me so desperately that I thought it better to ask the men to leave me to deal with the girl. After they had gone we sat together and I heard her story. She had had the most terrible year of illness and heartbreak. Her cries were just cries of anguish. I set up a time to see her later and with a friend we prayed with her through some of the things she told me about. The incident was a lesson to me of the importance of treating each person as an individual, loving them as Jesus did, and doing our best to preserve their dignity.

Probably the most releasing aspect of the ministry was knowing that this is God's work and not ours. We need to look for Him to show us how to minister and to leave the outcome with Him. There is no fixed way to pray for people, though being an orderly sort of person I would love to have a system to follow. There are helpful guidelines, such as the ones already outlined. But if we are trying to make Jesus our model for ministry, then He wasn't just loving and to the point, but He treated each person differently.

In Mark's gospel Jesus ministered to a blind man by taking him away from the crowd and putting mud on his eyes. Jesus prayed twice for him before he had full sight.[11] A few chapters later blind Bartimaeus received his sight. But this time Jesus didn't even appear to touch him and healed him with just a word.[12] The reason we invite the Holy Spirit to come when ministering to others is not because it's a bit of spiritual jargon, but because we are dependent on Him to show us the way to minister, and for the outcome. If that outcome is the one we have asked for, then to God be the glory. If nothing appears to happen, then we trust that God has blessed the person in ways we know nothing about.

In many instances we never know what God has done. But the privilege of getting older is that we have been around long enough to get feedback from people, sometimes many years after the event. A short while ago, I was doing an interview for a magazine. As the reporter got up to go, she told me that her sister had been healed at our church ten years previously of an enormous cyst on an ovary. The identity of the person who prayed for her would never be known, so God got all the glory.

In those early days we were on a steep learning curve and I am sure we made some errors, but knowing our own fallibility and weakness kept us humble. We learned not to presume that because we thought we had received a word of revelation that it was necessarily accurate and, in fact, it could be totally out of our own imaginations. So we began to learn to offer words of knowledge by saying, "I think God may be saying..." or even, "This may be totally wrong, and please test it, but I think God may be saying..."

With some words we would pray urgently for some wisdom as to how to offer them. On one occasion I was praying alongside another woman for a lady with arthritic hands. She was very crippled and in a lot of pain. We prayed for a while and then my partner whispered to me that she thought the lady had been molested by her father as a teenager. I remember feeling very reluctant to even suggest such a thing, but I trusted my friend. So I prayed urgently for wisdom and then I asked the lady with the crippled hands if she minded if we prayed through her relationship with her father. She nodded in agreement and so we prayed fairly generally, not mentioning the molestation. Almost immediately the lady began to weep and the tears fell on her outstretched hands. As they did so, her hands began to open up and before we had finished praying she was completely free of the arthritis. We never knew what had happened between her and her father. There was no need to know. It was enough that she had been healed.

In those early days we had some interesting situations which puzzled us. But God was teaching us how to manage the move of His Spirit without quenching Him. We were completely new in getting and giving words of revelation, but it was obvious that these were very helpful in discerning what God was doing. One member of the team was very responsive to the Holy Spirit, but at the same time quite a new Christian, so was in the process of getting healed up herself. Sometimes it was disturbing to minister alongside her because she would begin to cry out or make some strange movements, and then the ministry would move to praying for her. But after one of these occasions she told me she did not feel that it was she who needed the ministry, but that what was happening to her was for the other person. So instead of being put off by her strange reactions, I would ask her to describe what she was feeling. It was amazing. She was, in fact, receiving a word of knowledge about the person we were praying for, but in her immaturity, and ours, had not known how to pass it on.

One Sunday morning we were praying for a lady who was profoundly deaf and had come up in answer to a word of knowledge about a lifelong fear of small spaces. As we began to pray my young friend suddenly curled up in a ball and began to beat the air. On being questioned she said she felt as if she was closed in and trying to get out of a cupboard. We put the question to the deaf woman: "Have you ever been shut in a cupboard?" Light began to dawn and she slowly nodded her head and told us how, when she was a small child and had committed some misdemeanour, she had been shut in a cupboard by her nanny as a punishment. She also remembered hammering on the door in sheer panic. With her deafness already beginning to shut her off from others, it had been a traumatic experience for her.

Another thing that soon became obvious was that asking questions and stopping ministry to do so did not stop what God was doing, nor did making suggestions. On one occasion a woman was laid out on the floor making a very loud noise and those around were obviously bothered by it. David knelt beside her and said very quietly, "I can see that God is ministering to you and I want you to keep on receiving whatever God is doing with you, but did you realise that you were making rather a noise?"

"Am I?" she said. "I am so sorry."

Straight away she quietened down, but continued to be ministered to very effectively. It was on this occasion that David learned another important lesson in leading a traditional church when in the throes of a move of the Spirit. Because he had left the platform to deal with one particular disturbance, it had left the church without a visible leader. The congregation seemed able to cope with whatever happened, providing the person leading the service was still standing before them looking unperturbed.

It is good to remind ourselves now and again that though Jesus was infallible, we are not. Therefore we have to take care of how we minister to people and pray continually for love and wisdom. The gifts of the Spirit can be dangerous in careless hands. If St John were with us he would plead with us "to love one another," which means that now and again we need to stop and ask ourselves the questions, "Would I like this being done or said to me?" and "Is this the most loving way to minister to this person?"

Of course, healing is not just physical and though we started there, it slowly became obvious that Jesus was not only anointed to heal the sick, but as it says in Isaiah 61, the Lord had also anointed Him to *"bind up the broken hearted"* and to *"proclaim freedom for the captives"*. So the adventure in healing continued, developed and grew.

Endnotes:

1. Morphew, Dr Derek, *Breakthrough*, Vineyard International Publishers, 1991.
2. Matthew 12:28

3. Morphew, *Breakthrough*.

4. Revelation 21:4

5. Hebrews 2:8

6. Morphew, *Breakthrough*.

7. Luke 5:13

8. Luke 7:14

9. Mark 4:39

10. Luke 9:2, 10:9

11. Mark 8:23-25

12. Mark 10:46-52

13. 1 John 4:7

9
More Healing

When Jesus raised the dead, healed the sick and forgave sins, He was fulfilling Isaiah's prophecy *"to heal the broken hearted and proclaim freedom to the captives."*[1] Many that He healed had been prisoners to their sickness for many years before they were set free. Those who received back their dead had their hearts healed. But nowhere do we see Him "healing the broken hearted" in the way we practice the "inner healing" ministry today. The only place that He does anything similar is when He restores Peter.[2]

Peter, the impulsive, self-confident fisherman, who one moment declared Jesus to be the Messiah and the next is rebuked by Jesus when He talked about suffering and dying[3]; Peter the courageous disciple who declared to all the world that he would lay down his life for Jesus is the same person who, a few days later, denies Jesus to a little servant girl. Peter was outside in the courtyard, standing around a fire when Jesus was being cross-examined by Annas, father-in-law to the High Priest.

A girl challenged him as he warmed his hands:

"You are not one of his disciples are you?"

"I am not," he snapped back.

Three times he denies his relationship with Jesus.[4] Then the cock crowed and he broke down and wept.[5]

After the crucifixion the disciples went back to their fishing. It was morning and they had caught nothing. *"Early in the morning, Jesus stood on the shore, but the disciples did not realise it was Jesus."*[6] He instructed them to throw their net on the other side. When they did it they caught a large number of fish. It was a real *déjà vu* situation. At this point John recognised Jesus and told Peter who, as impulsive as ever, leapt from the boat stark naked and arrived at the shore before everyone else. Jesus had lit a fire and was cooking fish for breakfast.

When they had finished eating and were most likely relaxing around the fire, Jesus turned to Simon Peter and asked him three times, "Simon, do you love me?"[7] Three times Simon told Him that he did and three times Jesus re-commissioned him to feed the flock. The setting was very similar to the scene of Peter's denial – around a fire. The question is asked the same number of times – three. And then came the re-instatement. We can imagine how healing that re-commissioning was for Peter. But this seems to be the only place in the Bible where there is anything that comes close to our inner healing model, if one excludes deliverance from demons.

However, if we view inner healing as part of the process of maturity it is a perfectly biblical concept. The Bible is full of injunctions for us to mature, to grow up, and to be transformed into the image of Jesus. All of us are on a journey towards wholeness and maturity that extends from the day we first gave our hearts to Jesus until the day we see Him face to face.

But the process can be blocked for many different reasons: sin, unforgiveness, unresolved relationships, hurts from the past, misconceptions, and habitual behaviour patterns which are not particularly helpful, nor Christlike. Blockages need removing and sometimes these blockages are more easily resolved with help from others. In this context, inner healing is not only biblical, but necessary for all of us on our journey – though for most of us, it is achieved in the context of normal church life.

I recently heard of a young man who had started attending a home group in his local church. Obviously feeling at home with the group, he confessed to being a homosexual. The group continued to welcome and love him, even though they were clear as to what they felt was the biblical position on homosexuality. After two years of attending the group, he declared that he had given up this lifestyle and not only that, but he felt as if he had completely changed his orientation and was in the process of looking for a girlfriend. Over two years they had consistently accepted, loved and prayed with him – all of which should be normal practice in any good home group.

My first introduction to the inner healing ministry was with Fr. Frances McNutt while still in Chile, though I did not have the opportunity to see the ministry working first hand until we went to the Vineyard church in Anaheim. On that first visit, not only did we learn everything we could about the healing ministry and how the teams operated, but Carol Wimber and her sister Penny Fulton allowed me to sit in on several of their sessions with individual people who had more complicated problems than could be dealt with on a Sunday after a church service.

On another visit I was introduced to a personal growth course called "Free to Be" which they ran in their church. They generously gave me permission to take it home and use it as I wanted. I admit to having altered it quite a bit to fit an English audience. But the course was a huge success at St Andrew's and, in fact, for a number of years I led at least two courses a year. But it uncovered some quite deep issues in people's lives and I realised then that we would need to provide help for such people.

I had already begun to do the courses that were available at CWR (Crusade For World Revival) and they were extremely helpful. Selwyn Hughes was a superb teacher and I found him very challenging. One morning he taught us the pattern they used for ministry, after which we were set an uncomfortable task. One person was to be asked to be the counselee with a pretend problem and another was to be the counsellor. To my horror Selwyn turned to me for the counsellor's part. The session between the two of us would be filmed and the rest of the class would then make their comments as to how it had gone.

My immediate reaction was to say "No way, ask someone else!" But Selwyn looked me in the eye and asked me what was wrong with my self-esteem. "It's not good enough for that," I replied. But, of course, in the end I rose to the challenge. I think the rest of the class must have taken pity on me and I can't remember them being too critical. But it made me realise how delicate our self-esteem is. It is worth remembering that one of our greatest needs is for acceptance and one of our greatest fears is rejection.

Another time, Selwyn led us all in an imaginary journey down through the years of our lives. He started at about the age of 50 and worked backwards, taking ten years at a time. I admit to feeling a little shaky as we went through the time we spent in the church hall in Chile, but I managed to stay well in control – always important to me! But then he reached the age of ten and began to go down the staircase one year at a time. When he reached the age of three, there was a loud sound of sobbing and to my horror I realised it was me. Afterwards Richard and Prue Bedwell, who were both on the course, offered to pray with me. They had not been on the staff for long at that time and I was reluctant to open myself up to people I didn't know very well. So I politely dismissed their offer. However, a few months afterwards, trying to obey Jesus' injunction to first take the plank out of my eye before trying to help my brother or sister take the speck out of their eye,[8] I felt that I should be willing to deal with whatever in my life still needed resolution.

In fact, it was a very healing experience and one for which I shall always be grateful. The "hiccup" I had experienced on the imaginary journey was quickly diagnosed. My time in an isolation hospital with diphtheria happened when I was three and though I had not thought of it as particularly traumatic, I was aware that I had always had a horror of hospitals – in fact, even just visiting one would make me feel sick. Having been brought up in the evangelical tradition of *"forgetting what is behind and straining towards what is ahead"*[9] I had never delved into my past, and so had not connected this phobia with my childhood experience.

Going through a period of counselling myself was not just very healing, but a huge learning curve. I seemed to work on two levels. I was receiving whatever God was doing in my own life and, at the same time, noting the way in which I was being ministered to. So in one sense I was a guinea pig and in another a student in the school of learning.

By this time I had the bit between my teeth and was anxious to learn all I could which might be of help to us. Prue Bedwell and I began exploring every type of therapeutic help, both for groups and individuals. We had some very strange experiences along the way. One I remember well was a secular "Gestalt" weekend to explore attachment and separation. On our way to the first evening I said that I thought we ought to keep a low profile. But to my dismay, when we were split into pairs to tell each other our similarities and differences, Prue explained to her partner that she thought probably one of the major differences was the fact that she was a Christian. Oh, dear, the cat was among the pigeons!

The whole weekend took a turn that the poor leader had never anticipated, which was to do with our attachment to and separation from God. I remember one young man whose turn it was to vent some feelings, beating up an unsuspecting pillow in rage at God. I didn't feel comfortable letting this pass and suggested he might direct his feelings at the real cause of his anger, which I suspected, from the things he had already shared, was his own father. For one moment I thought he was going to hit me instead of the pillow. It was a memorable weekend!

Gradually, out of the healing team, trained and authorised by David, we began to pick members of that team who were mature Christians with a good biblical knowledge, who had the time and ability to see people for more in depth ministry. We were fortunate in having a number of retired couples who proved to be a great help and over about twelve years faithfully prayed with numbers of people. They were especially useful when we began having clergy retreats based at the church. The visitors would have formal sessions with the staff of the church, but would stay in various homes for the ten days where they were able to receive ministry from their hosts. Even to this day, twenty years later, I meet clergy who look back on that time of ministry as a turning point in their lives.

Prue and I did the teaching for the Pastoral Prayer Team, which was how it became known. Richard was the one behind the scenes who organised the days and was in fact the co-ordinator for the ministry. We started that day with teaching on the boundaries and guidelines and finished with the values. Though it might have appeared to the participants to be the less interesting part of the day, in my mind those two sessions were the most important.

One of our highest values was the work of the Holy Spirit. What we were all learning was to follow His leading by inviting Him to come and then lead the ministry. So though we gave a loose pattern for ministry which people could bear in mind, we did not want to make it into a system, remembering that Jesus treated each individual differently. The other values were all important, such as love for the individual, authority in the name of Jesus, the work of Christ on the cross, the Word of God, the growth of the individual and the body of Christ. The values under-girded the ministry and we knew that if the team kept them in mind they would not go far wrong. The boundaries and guidelines were a little different. They were a bit like the rules of engagement. Anyone who wanted to be part of the team had to agree to them. We had learned through our mistakes and didn't want to bring such an important, but potentially damaging ministry, into disrepute, nor hurt a vulnerable human being.

Early on I had been praying with a young woman in what we used to term 'the upper room". It was a room at the top of the building and far from the parish offices. It had the advantage of being quiet and undisturbed. I was on my own and half way through the prayer time the young girl I was praying with launched herself towards me and landed on my lap, totally taking me by surprise. I tried desperately to disentangle myself, but she clung on and for a while I was trapped. At around the same time as this happened to me, Prue was trapped in her own house by a large girl who turned out to be a lesbian and decided she didn't want to leave. Prue eventually had to phone Richard and he came back from the office to remove the angry person.

From that day on I decided that in a church setting, this type of ministry was best done in twos. It was our first guideline and one we kept to strictly from then on. It was explained to each counselee that there would be three people in the confidentiality circle: Richard, who did the first interview and who would only know the barest details, and two others who would perform the ministry. No one, to my knowledge, ever objected to seeing two people. It also had the advantage of lessening the likelihood of dependency occurring, though inevitably there was always an element of this. No one tells another their deepest feelings, both good and bad, without making an attachment to those who have listened to them and empathised with them, but it was not difficult to manage with two people involved.

Another guideline was timing. No one was to see a person after 10.30 at night nor for longer than about 1½ hours. People in pain can be quite manipulative and demanding. So often I would find that a person would sit in silence for an hour, at which point we would call the session to a halt. Only then would they start to open up. As we usually had another person waiting, or husbands hoping for a meal, we would bring the session to a close in the knowledge that next time they would be quicker in getting to the point. It is never wise to minister late into the night. We have an enemy, Satan, who would love to tire the brethren out so that they find the job of helping to set the captives free too demanding and decide to give it up. In particular, demons have a way of manifesting at a late hour and will keep the saints up until late if they can.

Not only does the enemy try and exhaust us with late nights, but so often taps into our own needs or unhealed places. For this reason we encouraged the team to be open to ministry themselves before trying to minister to others. Obviously, the members of the

team were not all healed up. We would never have had a team if
we had had to wait for that to happen. But it was important they
were open to ministry and on the road to wholeness, as well as
being fairly self-aware.

There is safety in people who know themselves, especially those
who are aware of their weaknesses. For example, those who
are compulsive "rescuers" but think that their need to rescue is
being like Jesus are a danger in ministry. Jesus was a rescuer *par
excellence*, but what drove Him was the will of His Father. His food
was to do the will of Him who sent Him.[10] If anything compelled
Him it was that. He was not driven by the needs of those around
Him. If He had been He would not have been able to move on to
another village, leaving needy people behind, nor would He have
only healed one person at the pool of Bethesda where there was
a multitude of sick people.[11]

The compulsive rescuer, however, is compelled by the need to
rescue and doesn't wait to find out God's agenda in the situation.
This instinct usually comes out of a childhood experience of being
placed in the role of helper for a prolonged period and gradually
it becomes an identity – a way of life. The tendency then is to
be so continually giving out to others that "burn out" follows.
Another danger is that those who are being rescued may be kept
in an immature place for too long and not encouraged to take
responsibility and grow up.

When Richard began to co-ordinate the ministry he challenged
me on how many people I had been seeing, both with Prue and
with others. I knew he was right and that my list was too long. I
assured him I would cut back, but that week I took on another
person and couldn't think why I had done it. I was beginning to
feel exhausted. That Sunday there was a general time of ministry.
David had us all standing and invited the Holy Spirit to come. Those

who felt they wanted to pray for others moved around and prayed briefly over anyone on whom the Spirit seemed to be resting. I was standing engaged with God when a young girl came up and laid her hands on me. Immediately, I saw in my mind's eye a huge pool. I remember feeling as if I was carrying a very heavy burden and that the pool was the tears of all those broken people who seemed to demand my attention. In my imagination I walked up to the pool and to my dismay saw my own reflection in it. Instantly, I knew the pool was full of my own tears.

As I reflected on this picture I realised that, though I am not a compulsive rescuer, I have a problem saying "no" to people who use the words, "I need you." When I was a child I was often left on my own and sometimes, when I needed an adult, there seemed to me to be no one there. Somewhere along the line I must have said to myself that I wouldn't let anyone else be in that position. So when someone said those three little words to me, my immediate desire was to be there for them. It was a typical case of transference where a person unconsciously redirects feelings away from themselves and on to another. The pain was mine and I was placing it on others who may or may not have been feeling the feelings I was crediting them with. Just knowing this was happening gave me the power to choose and not just be swept along.

First, I ceased taking my diary to church, which meant people had to phone me on another day if they wanted to see me, which gave me time to pray and take stock. Then, when they phoned, I would first ask the nature of their problem. So often it was nothing urgent and did not need immediate attention. I might not even have been the appropriate person to see. It felt so much better not to be compelled to respond to everyone who appeared to need me.

In some circles there seems to be a "quick fix" mentality. It is natural to want one's problems to go away quickly, but maturity comes as we work at issues in our lives.   One of the quick fixes we met was "healing of the memories". Though a wonderful discovery, it could be superficial. Just to have Jesus walk back through a memory and heal the trauma of it was, in my opinion, to leave a person only marginally better off. As I have stated, the only way I was able to see inner healing as a biblical concept was if it was put it in the context of maturity and being transformed into the image of Jesus. If something in a person's past was blocking that growth, then it needed a resolution. But even then I found that just resolving the trauma by forgiveness, though a necessary part of healing, was not enough. The consequences of the trauma needed dealing with. The person's thinking would most likely be skewed as a result and because our thinking leads to behaviour then that also needed looking at.

Secondly, another "quick fix" solution that many people went chasing after was deliverance. I remember several people from the church would disappear for a weekend and come back having had numerous demons cast out, including such ones as depression, grief, anger and even smoking. They were convinced that their problems were over, and so it appeared for a few weeks, but before long it was apparent that nothing had really changed. This is not to say that we did not believe that demons existed, nor were unwilling to deal with them when they appeared. There are many stories we could tell of real demons manifesting and people being wonderfully delivered. But that has been only the beginning of the journey for such people. They may still need healing, renewal of the mind and behaviour change and those things are not accomplished in a weekend.

Something I have noticed with demonization is that true

repentance usually means the person is freed very easily and quickly. On one occasion Prue and I were in a session with a young girl in her early twenties. She had recently come back to the Lord after a disastrous period away in the far country. She spent the first half an hour making a full confession of all that she had been into. Some of it was pretty lurid and of a particularly nasty sexual nature. She didn't spare us the details, but told her story with tears and obvious repentance. When we came to pray with her we first invited the Holy Spirit to come and lead us in the ministry. As we did so she made a strange face. I looked at Prue and she looked at me and we raised our eyebrows. I was sure we were in the presence of an unclean spirit and from her story I wasn't surprised.

Not wanting to scare the young woman unnecessarily I spoke to any darkness within her and told it to be gone in the name of Jesus. I remember she shook her head and then opened her eyes and said, "What was that? I feel so light." I am sure that whatever was hanging around could not stay in the presence of the Holy Spirit and her real repentance.

Week by week people from around the area came to the church wanting prayer and many asked for appointments with our team for further prayer. However, we made a decision that though we were always willing to pray for people who came to a Sunday service or a celebration, we were not taking on folk from other churches for Pastoral Prayer ministry. Every church is responsible for the pastoral care of its own members and in any case we had almost more than we could manage. But we did suggest that other churches sent along teams to our training days and we would help them set up a similar prayer team.

The eighties and nineties were a wonderful season in the life of many churches. It was exciting to see God on the move in some amazing ways in people's lives. We had our critics, however, who questioned whether anything beneficial was achieved during that time. We have had the privilege of being in the same church for nineteen years and another fifteen years living in the same area. It means that David and I have had the opportunity of seeing the results of the blessing in people's lives.

David explains that any dramatic encounter with the Holy Spirit maybe termed "crisis". This is followed by "process", when there appears to be very little happening, but in fact the Holy Spirit is processing what has happened and bringing maturity. Then finally there is "fruitfulness", when we see the result of what God has been doing in the "crisis" and the "process".

A story that David is fond of telling is of a man who came to the church because his daughter told him he should. He had been thrown out of the house by his wife and had been sleeping rough in his car. Several times he said that he tried to come into the church but something prevented him. He eventually made it and encountered the power of God for the first time in his life. David found him lying on the floor begging God to stop whatever He was doing, because he couldn't stand any more. He became a regular member and was often found on the floor under the anointing of the Holy Spirit. He was eventually remarried to a woman in the church who had had a similarly dramatic encounter with God. Though they had little money between them they raised enough to go with another couple from the church on a trip to India. Since then they have gone every year over a period of about ten years and have set up schools, baptised believers, ordained pastors and helped build churches. *Crisis*, *process* then, to God be the glory, *fruitfulness*.

When we retired in 1996, though we joined the Soul Survivor Church in Watford we could not be regular members. Retirement meant we were free to travel, speak more, and do things together. So the call of God moved on. I was no longer working in the same way out of a local church and the inner healing ministry, to be safe and wholesome, needs to be based in a local church context. However, I did begin to see people on an ad hoc basis for mentoring. This caused me to think more about the subject of personal growth which every Christian is involved in. I wanted to help people who had no recourse to in-depth ministry in their local church, but still had to work at any blockages or problems they might encounter along the way.

The call of God changes with our circumstances, but whatever our age, wherever we live, it behoves us all to seek God for the next part of His plan for our lives.

Endnotes:

1. Isaiah 61:1
2. John 21:4-25
3. Mark 8:27-33
4. John 18:15-27
5. Mark 14:72
6. John 21:4
7. John 21:15-17
8. Matthew 7:5
9. Philippians 3:13
10. John 4:34
11. John 5:2

10
More Change

1996 was the year of David's bombshell. He was 65 and ready to retire! My immediate reaction was purely selfish. I wasn't ready. But in marriage one's lives are tied together, like it or not. I had had three years as a curate's wife, seventeen years as a missionary wife and nineteen years as a vicar's wife – so when the inevitable happened, I felt totally disorientated. "Who am I now?" was the question I kept asking myself.

Retirement didn't feel like anything in particular. These feelings were a surprise to me. I hadn't realised how much my identity was tied into David's work and I knew some soul searching lay ahead. So began a journey of discovery, at the end of which I wrote a book called, *Who Am I?* Only gradually did I begin to sense the next season in God's call on my life.

Dealing with the blockages and discovering the aids to personal growth, in one sense, had been foundational to the inner healing ministry that I had been involved in for so many years, but as I explored the subject of identity, I realised what a huge unresolved area this was for many people and getting it sorted could be a real aid to growth. I sensed that concentrating on personal growth was a natural progression in the journey that God had been taking me along. This led to the making of two DVDs on *maturity* (The Road to Maturity and Marks of Maturity – see back of book for details).

Because we were now members of a Youth Church I had the opportunity to chat with many of the young people there and hear their stories. It was amazing how many were saying in different ways that they didn't know who they really were. As one young man put it, "I feel like one person on the outside and another on the inside. On the outside I look as if I have it all together, but on the inside I feel so weak and vulnerable. Who am I really?"

Around that time I watched an episode of the famous "Brat Camp" programme on Channel 4. I was shocked by the behaviour and language of the young girls sent out from England by their parents to the Utah desert. It was a last ditch attempt at changing their self-destructive behaviour. One sixteen-year old girl confessed to the American therapist that she was a regular cannabis user. "That's who I am," she repeated several times. I think she was really saying that she had lost her identity to such an extent that she only felt she had found herself when she was in a drug-induced haze. As I watched, amazed at such a sad and terribly mistaken admission, I wondered what had gone wrong in that poor girl's life to have caused her to lose herself in such a dramatic way.

Identity is made up of various building blocks which are the same for us all. The first sense we have of "self" comes through our attachments. We know ourselves through our mother's and father's eyes. If they are happy with us, we feel happy. It becomes an "I'm okay" identity. Gradually that expands and we become "our mother's/father's daughter/son" or someone's sister or brother, and so on. For many, this is a good experience and therefore the first block in their identity is happily in position. But there are those for whom it is a painful aspect of their identity and one which they would rather forget.

Another building block is the time in which we live and the place where we are born and grow up. I grew up in Devon and as a child I was often called a "Devonshire Dumpling" due to my rosy cheeks. By the time I was three we were a country at war and so to add to my identity I was also a "war baby". Though it is still true that these two elements form a part in how I see myself, now, after so many years, it is only a small part. However, whenever David waxes eloquent about the wonders of Suffolk I can feel the Devonshire Dumpling coming to life! Though this building block may be unseen it can still affect me. North Devon is largely a rural community and after all these years I can find myself feeling frustration and anger rising up within me for the plight of the farmers. I was almost ready to march to support the rural community against the hunting ban. Our roots may seem unimportant and in the past, but they will continue exerting an influence upon us throughout our life.

The next building block is experience – both good and bad. Students of the brain tell us that we tend to remember those things that have strong emotional content attached to them, whether positive or negative. So the very happy experiences are lodged there to be forever a part of who we are, but so too are the unhappy ones. We may try to forget the negative happenings, but while they remain unresolved they will tend to make their presence felt by not only becoming more influential than they should be, but with a tendency to obscure the good memories. Once resolved, however, they lose their old power over us.

Another building block in our identity comes from the opinions others have of us. It used to be said that "sticks and stones can break my bones, but words can never hurt me." How untrue that is. The words said over us as children can become indelibly printed upon our psyche. In the beginning, children are like clean slates. They are totally dependent on those around them to fill it and to give them information about who they are. Their "I am" worldview begins to form from the first day of their life onwards. Those careless words that were said in anger may hurt at the time, but it is the ones repeated many times that stick and damage the emerging self.

Similarly, the positive opinions need to be reinforced over time for them to be positively influential. The years of childhood are tremendously important in forming identity. Opinions, first from our parents, then the wider family circle, our teachers and eventually peers may all exert their power over a lifetime. I remember a middle-aged, family man explaining to us that he was a failure. When we asked him why he held such an opinion of himself, he explained quite seriously that he "just was". But on further questioning we could find no reason for this assumption. He had a perfectly good job, a happy marriage and two lovely children.

Apparently that was what his father had told him from an early age – and children, like blotting paper, soak up all that adults say to them. His father's opinion seemed to be indelibly printed upon his mind, regardless of his circumstances. I am reminded of the man who said that for the first fifteen years of his life he thought his name was "shut up". Sadly, there is a feeling abroad that nagging and criticising a child will make him or her do better. Studies have shown that, in the average home, for every positive statement, a child will receive ten negative ones. And the school environment is not much better. Students apparently hear seven negative statements from their teachers for every one positive statement.[1] This shows that this particular building block may be more negative than positive for many people.

We live in a world that puts a high premium on success. How often have we heard young aspiring pop idols or football stars say that success "means everything to me"? We think that by becoming famous we will feel like a person who matters at last. Usually inside a person who yearns to be a "somebody" is a person who feels like a "nobody". Clearly what we do is a significant building block of our lives, but it can become more significant for our sense of identity than it ever should. One of my daughters lived for a time in a university town and because of her husband's job she attended many of the university functions. She was inevitably asked what her job was. When she replied that she was "a stay at home mum" her reply was greeted with shock. No longer do we realise that "the hand that rocks the cradle rules the world".

So if these are the building blocks of our identity, what is the cement that holds them together? In my studies on identity I discovered that to have a healthy, solid sense of self we need three things to be present:[2] The first is "continuity". In other words, we have to have an identity that is stable and unchanging – difficult to achieve in our ever-changing world. I remember a young girl coming to see me because she was feeling very depressed and as a consequence had been laid off work. Within just a few months she had left college, left home, got married and then started a new job. There had been too many changes in too short a short space of time and she felt as if she had lost herself in all the moves.

The second element is "differentiation". We want to feel that in some sense we are unique or special and not just an insignificant nonentity in a crowd.

Thirdly is a sense of "value". These three are the cement that holds the building blocks of identity in place. But when we take time to consider the building blocks mentioned, not one of them fulfils all three criteria completely.

Attachments are by their nature unreliable. People come and go in our lives. Other people's opinions of us vary. Experiences are ever changing and our activity and achievements change with the years. As for our sense of individuality and distinctiveness, this is hard to achieve in our computerised "virtual" society. Steve Turner's poem, *The Proof* says it all:

Do you have any identification?
Diner's Card?
Access?
American Express?
Bank Statement?
Driving Licence?
Then I am sorry, sir,
You do not exist?

The numerous Internet-based chat rooms that have sprung up in recent years give us all the opportunity to be exactly who we want to be and project any personality we like. But there is no true differentiation here, nor continuity. As for a sense of value, some very fortunate individuals have had the privilege of having been nurtured in an environment of encouragement and positive affirmation, which has left them with good self-esteem.

But sadly too few have had such an experience. So we are left with seemingly irresolvable identity issues. But, as I discovered, there is more! The above are all to do with the here and now. An identity which has been formed in time should be seen as insignificant compared with one forged in eternity – the one that will last forever.

Henri Nouwen puts it so well in his book, *Life of the Beloved*:

"Our preciousness, uniqueness and individuality are not given to us by those who meet us in clock time – our brief chronological existence – but by the One who has chosen us with an everlasting love, a love that existed from all eternity and will last through all eternity."[3]

As I had found out, to my consternation, if we attach our identity to another person or to some sort of activity we are bound to flounder and feel, as I did for a time, quite disorientated. But my journey of discovery was well worth the effort as I discovered the glorious truth of who I was in Christ. This identity is unchanging, individual and imputes us with an amazing value – one that we could certainly never earn. The identity which has been forged in "clock time", is real, and there is nothing wrong with the building blocks we have mentioned, but it's not all there is. There is another truth operating and we all have a choice as to which one we live from.

It is worth picking out the verses of Scripture which spell out our eternal identity and then spending time basking in those truths:

"How great is the love the Father has lavished on us, that we should be called children of God! And that is what we are!" (1 John 3:1)

"But you are a chosen people, a royal priesthood, a holy nation, a people belonging to God." (1 Peter 2:9)

"...God's chosen people, holy and dearly loved..." (Colossians 3:12)

"For we are God's workmanship, created in Christ Jesus to do good works, which God prepared in advance for us to do." (Ephesians 2:10)

"For we are to God the aroma of Christ among those who are being saved and those who are perishing." (2 Corinthians 2:15)

We are more than we ever imagined and the choice is ours as to which identity we chose to live in and live out. We can listen to the world with all its negativity and success-obsessed culture and can be easily caught in its deceptive trap. As Henri Nouwen so aptly writes,

"As long as we allow our parents, siblings, teachers, friends and lovers to determine whether we are chosen or not, we are caught in the net of a suffocating world that accepts or rejects us according to its own agenda of effectivity and control."[4]

Or we can choose to listen to the voice of One who loves us with an everlasting love and has a wonderful purpose and plan for each of our lives. Paul encourages us to, *"fix our eyes not on what is seen but on what is unseen, for what is seen is temporary, but what is unseen is eternal."*[5]

But we may need encouragement to persevere in our God-given identity. Henri Nouwen gives us some practical tips on living in the truth of who we are in Christ.

First, we must keep unmasking the world around us. It is too easy to allow their standards and values to infiltrate our thinking. The culture around us can slowly poison us unawares. I remember back in the '80s, Roy Castle, a well known musician, died of lung cancer. He had never smoked a cigarette in his life, but as a young man he had played in men's clubs up and down the country. He must have inhaled the smoke that had filled the atmosphere in such places. Similarly, we easily absorb the world's culture. To combat this we must keep coming back to biblical values and priorities.

Secondly, we must continually remind ourselves of God's identity for us.

Thirdly, Henri Nouwen suggests we should celebrate our choseness on a daily basis. It is easy to know that truth with our minds, but not to live as if it were true.

Lastly, we should look for the people and places where God's truth is spoken. Many of us work in non-Christian environments and we need friends who will encourage us to live as chosen, beloved, children of God. We need people around us who know us well enough to challenge us when we have slipped back into an old negative identity. Such friends are absolutely indispensable as we try to walk in the truth of who we are in Christ. We were not created to be alone. Friendship is a God-given bonus to our lives.

Endnotes:

1. Anderson, Neil T., Victory Over The Darkness, Monarch, 1990.
2. Breakwell, Glynis, Coping With Threatened Identities, Methuen, 1986.
3. Nouwen, Henri J M., Life of the Beloved, Hodder and Stoughton, 1992.
4. Ibid.
5. 2 Corinthians 4:18

11
Friendship

When I married David there was an unspoken rule in the Church that clergy did not have close friends in the parish. This meant that either one's friends were on the staff or lived at a distance. Not having had a church background I found this very frustrating, though in the early weeks of marriage I imagined that my relationship with David would be quite enough for me. But after a month or so I realised that David was busy in the parish and I was left for many hours twiddling my thumbs. As our Vicar didn't like his curate's wives to work I was often lonely and bored. It was a relief to move on to a second curacy where David was in charge of a daughter church and it seemed natural to become friends with several couples there of our own age. By this time I was pregnant and within a year of marriage had a small baby to care for and as most first-time mothers will appreciate, she took up a great deal of time which didn't leave much space for any in depth relationships, apart from David.

David and I had become friends about three years before we were married. I was the secretary of the Young People's Group in the church and as he was the curate, this was a group he was in charge of. We painted the church room together, organised and went on rambles, played tennis and did all the other things that those groups do. We found we were stimulated by each other's company, but at the time neither of us felt marriage was the way forward.

Looking back I think we were both a little bit naïve. At the time David had in his mind someone a little different from me. She would be a girl from a missionary background or at least from a keen Christian family, whereas my family were business people who didn't go to church and had never even met a missionary. So we plumped for friendship. And that is how it stayed for the next three years. But little by little the friendship deepened and began to be increasingly necessary to both of us. We couldn't imagine a future that didn't feature our relationship.

During those years we frequently shared our lunchtimes together. There were some very cheap restaurants in Oxford and most days we would meet at one of them for bangers and beans, usually to discuss the young people's group.

One day we were eating lunch and David announced that he was moving out of his digs and into a flat of his own, but he lacked several things and would I mind helping him buy some saucepans. So off we went to the nearest hardware store. We walked in and the assistant came up and asked how he could help us.

"I need some saucepans," said David.

"How big is the family, sir?" asked the young man.

At this point David turned to me and asked, without even a twinkle in his eye, how many I would like. I was completely taken by surprise, but responded quickly: "How about a dozen?"

"That's fine," said David and with that we bought the saucepans.

I went back to my job, which by this time was in the County Children's Department; - work much more to my liking than the tax office. I told my boss that I wasn't sure, but I thought I might have just received a proposal of marriage. And so it turned out. The next time we met David was talking about the wedding.

I have to admit to feeling a little defrauded of that romantic proposal which other girls I knew had received. However, when we went down to Devon to see my parents we took a walk one afternoon and stopped by a five-bar gate where I requested that David do the job properly. So down on one knee he went and I received the sort of proposal I had always dreamed of! Then he opened his little New Testament and read Roman 8, which starts with "no condemnation" and ends with "no separation". It has ever after been a favourite passage of mine. And that was how I came to marry my best friend.

Sadly, in today's world couples often move on too quickly to the level of physical intimacy and don't have the joy of exploring each other's personalities and laying the foundation of friendship first. Without that, what is there when the romance has worn off? Those three years were a good beginning, but after that we had the advantage of being thrown together even more closely and having to lean heavily on one another in Chile. David has worked from our home nearly all our lives and though he may be busy, nevertheless he has been around a good deal. So in many ways we have been very fortunate in being able to maintain the closeness. However, this did not mean it was an exclusive relationship. We both needed other people.

Everyone needs friendship. Whether we are married or single we need closeness with one or two people who know us through and through. Most of us have many acquaintances with whom it is easy to pass the time of day, but sadly, at the end of the day, these may never fill the need of closeness that we all have.

There are many factors which keep us from enjoying a closer type of relationship. I think the cyber age in which we live encourages social networking that can take up hours of time, but never involves any real face to face communication. Many opt for this easy way out of their loneliness, though it doesn't involve commitment or sacrifice of any sort. It's a false intimacy or pseudo-friendship, but tricks us into thinking we have lots of friends.

Someone told me just the other day that he had over a hundred friends on Facebook. These are just names on a computer screen and in no way do they represent the type of relationship which can provide comfort, support and challenge. However, having said that I am grateful for email. It enables me to keep in touch with my friends overseas. I have one friend who lives in Chile and with whom I either talk on the phone or email every week, sometimes twice a week. We try and visit twice a year. David and I go there once a year and she comes here once a year. But this relationship started as a face-to-face one and was one in which we met almost every day for about seven years. Now the only way we can continue it is through the modern invention of the Internet and the not so modern telephone. But with the real friendship of the past to build on it is still very meaningful.

Sometimes it is the commitment we fear. We think that such closeness will take up too much time, energy and effort. We live in a frantic world where, for all the mod-cons, we never have enough time. We rush from place to place and fear that one more commitment would take up time we just don't have. Sadly, this may be true, but the prospect is a lonely old age.

A middle-aged lady confessed to me recently that she didn't have close friends because she knew she had built a wall around herself so that no one could come in close enough to hurt her. Past let-downs and hurts can leave their mark upon us and, almost without realising, we may be drawing back from closeness out of fear of being let down all over again. However, whatever the cause, relationships are vital to our wellbeing and our lives will be the poorer for lack of them.

God lives in relationship (Father, Son and Holy Spirit – Three in One) and He created us to live the same way. He looked at Adam on his own and said, *"It is not good for man to be alone."*[1] And He created Eve to be his companion. There are many illustrations of great friendships in the Bible, the most famous one being that of David and Jonathan. David's lament when Jonathan and Saul died is heartbreaking. But his sorrow for Jonathan is over the loss of his best friend.

"How the mighty have fallen in battle! Jonathan lies slain on your heights. I grieve for you, Jonathan my brother, you were very dear to me. Your love for me was wonderful, more wonderful than that of women..."[2]

Ruth and Naomi are another illustration of a close relationship which was so enriching and beneficial to them both, and which in the beginning involved great sacrifice on the part of Ruth, who left her home and country to go with Naomi. Then In the book of Ecclesiastes we read the famous passage about friendship:

"Two are better than one, because they have a good return for their work: If one falls down his friend can help him up. But pity the man who falls and has no one to help him up! Also, if two lie down together, they will keep warm. But how can one keep warm alone? Though one may be overpowered, two can defend themselves. A cord of three strands is not quickly broken."[3]

This passage speaks of the enormous benefits of friendship, the first being a good return for their work. Jesus was so wise when He sent His disciples out two by two. My desire not to bother other people and to be independent has sometimes been my downfall. Two occasions stand out in my mind.

One was an invitation to a women's meeting in London. I reasoned to myself that it was only at the end of the railway line and therefore it would be no problem to go up on my own. However, it didn't turn out to be that easy. First the train was held up and I began to fret that I was going to be late. Having been a very punctual person all my life this did nothing for my anxiety level. I eventually reached my destination and was put up to speak almost immediately. At the end of my talk a queue of women formed, all wanting either to talk to me or to be prayed for. Being on my own I proceeded to do this throughout the lunch hour until I finally managed to tear myself away at about 2.30pm. I had been on my feet for four hours! If I had had the sense to take one of my friends, she would have shared the ministry and also made sure I had a break for lunch.

I thought I had learned my lesson until about two years later when I was asked to do a women's meeting in a town quite close by. I ascertained that it would take me no more than 30 minutes to get there. The route looked fairly simple, so I decided not to ask anyone to accompany me.

What a mistake! On the way I took a wrong turning and found myself going up the M1 at great speed in the wrong direction. I turned around as soon as I was able, but I had lost about 15 minutes. Now I was on a route I had not planned and very soon I was hopelessly lost. I kept stopping and asking directions and little by little found the place, but not until I had nearly died of anxiety and given the lady running the meeting a heart attack! On neither occasion was there a good return for my work. I had not been able to give 100% and instead of coming away rejoicing I arrived home feeling depressed at my own stupid independence. Two are definitely better than one!

Friendship also provides a steadying presence. I would never have survived our time in Chile, especially in the early days, without David's positive outlook and constant reminders that God had called us and therefore He would look after us. I remember after the 1960 earthquake hearing the rumours that the Andes mountains were gradually pushing Chile into the Pacific Ocean. My immediate reaction was to either pack up and go home now or build a boat in readiness. But David, with male logic, explained that even if the rumours were true it would be hundreds of years before the place where we lived would eventually succumb to that kind of pressure.

The verses also speak of two keeping each other warm. As I write, the weather this winter has been extremely cold and I know that statement to be true. King David suffered from the cold when he grew old and so his servants found him a young virgin named Abishag to lay beside him and keep him warm.

But in the case of my friends I think more in terms of the emotional support they have provided. In counselling the word "dependency" causes a counsellor to shudder, but in friendship there has to be some interdependence or closeness which would be sorely missed if it were not there. Eleanor Roosevelt said that many people will walk in and out of your life, but only true friends will leave footprints in your heart. Those footprints mean that the relationship has stood the test in all types of situations.

There is often a cost attached to being there for another person as an emotional support. A few years ago David and I were visiting Chile and David was taken ill in the middle of the night with a serious bladder infection and we needed to get to a hospital urgently. We didn't have the usual NHS medical support around us and it was a very worrying experience. My friend, Anderly, with whom we were staying was amazing. She travelled with us the two hours to a hospital in the capital, stayed with me throughout the night and, for the next three days, she didn't leave my side until David was released. Instinctively she knew that as independent as I appear, at that moment I desperately needed all the support she could give me.

I love the poem about friendship by Billy Sprague:

A friend should be drastic
He should go over the edge when you are in a pinch,
Stand firm when you are wrong and not budge an inch
And carry your burden with barely a flinch.
And a friend should be gymnastic.
He should muscle you up when you stumble
Balance the facts when you grumble
And flip into praise when you're humble.
But most of all
A friend should be elastic
He should expand your horizons,
Stretch your imagination,
Tighten your morals,
But loosen your limitations.
He should snap back to your side when the world turns mean,
And bend over backwards to believe in your dreams.

As I think about my friends, especially David, I have been the beneficiary of all the above.

Oprah Winfrey was being interviewed recently by Piers Morgan and he asked her about her friendship with Gayle King, with whom she has worked for years. Oprah became quite emotional and said that she would wish that every person in the world would have a friend like Gayle to care for them and be known by them, in such a way that they only wanted the best for their friend.[4] Friendship has been highly valued down through the ages. Cicero said (in about 50BC) that life is nothing without friendship and Francis Bacon said that the worst solitude is to be destitute of sincere friendship.

The benefit of friendship is not just the comfort it gives. If it is a good, healthy relationship it will also present a challenge. The Bible also encourages us to speak the truth in love to one another.[5] So often this is used by those who don't truly love us. But if a correction is given from someone we know loves us and is committed to our wellbeing, though difficult to swallow, the criticism can be very beneficial and growth producing. The writer of Proverbs tells us that the wounds of a friend can be trusted.[6] Proverbs also speaks of the sharpening that can take place in such a relationship. *"As iron sharpens iron, so one man sharpens another."*[7]

Lee Strobel is an investigative reporter. He would have described himself as an atheist until one day he was stunned when his wife Leslie announced that she had become a Christian. He had married a fun-loving, risk-taking, carefree woman. Now he had to brace himself for the worst. But instead he was genuinely impressed by the difference in his wife. He was fascinated by the fundamental changes in her character, her integrity and her personal confidence.

Eventually, he wanted to get to the bottom of what was prompting these subtle but significant shifts in his wife's attitude, so he launched into an all-out investigation into the facts surrounding the case for Christianity. His search led him to find the real Jesus and he became a Christian. The changes in his wife had challenged him to look seriously at the claims of Jesus and subsequently write some very helpful books such as *The Case for Christ*[8] and *The Case for a Creator*.[9]

Friendship is one of God's gifts to us and should be treated carefully but celebrated with gratitude. Someone has said that friends are God's way of looking after us. However, as with every good gift, we have an enemy who wants to ruin it for us. It is good for us to know the traps that it is possible to fall into that can mess up a good relationship.

I think the most common one is *possessiveness*, which leads to exclusivity and jealousy. If this enters a relationship it can quickly turn sour and shrivel. Why does it happen? Usually it springs out of insecurity. If that insecurity remains a part of the relationship then those difficult feelings can easily begin to spoil it.

I was chatting recently with a friend and she was laughing about the painful feelings of threat she had experienced in the early days of our relationship every time I spent time with someone else. Those feelings subsided gradually because firstly, she didn't give in to them or act them out, and secondly, when she realised that I was truly committed to a friendship with her.

When a relationship becomes tainted by moody silences and angry accusations the writing is on the wall. The only way it can be rescued is if the reactions are recognised and confessed as being unhealthy and detrimental to the relationship. Then two directions are possible: the friendship may come to an end or the roots of the insecurity being uncovered may lead to healing.

If the latter route is taken then the relationship has a future. Usually the insecurity arises from a past experience of being let down or hurt by someone close and this is where the healing is needed. After this, the work begins of changing the unhealthy, destructive and probably habitual responses. As someone has so wisely said, "Insanity is doing the same thing over again and expecting to get something different back." Friendship has to be worked at. It doesn't usually come on a plate.

Another trap one can fall into is that of *expectations*. People vary in their interpretations of commitment. One person thinks this means spending every spare moment together and another thinks that it means meeting on a fairly regular basis. The only way through this is to discuss it openly. Ask each other what each is expecting from the relationship. If it is to continue and grow into something worthwhile and beneficial to both parties then compromise will be needed. Compromise calls for sacrifice.

However, there has to be a proportional level of sacrifice. If it is one-sided then it might work initially, but it tends to sour with time. On holiday I would lay by a pool and read all day if I had it my way, but David doesn't like swimming or the sun. He likes to go and have coffee somewhere and do some sightseeing. So we compromise. I go sightseeing with him for part of the time and other days I lay in the sun while he sits in the shade.

One of the most unhealthy traps that friends can fall into is where one is a *rescuer* and the other is *needy*. This usually ends in disaster. After a while the rescuer feels he/she is being taken for granted or the one being rescued begins to want space to grow. Either way, the relationship usually ends in some frustrated recriminations. If this doesn't happen, it may just remain in a static place of unhealthy co-dependence, with each playing out their neurosis on the other. The best model for any friendship is interdependence, where support is given and received in equal measure.

Friendship outside of marriage can be enriching, but only when it is inclusive of the marriage partner. The danger arises when it becomes exclusive and all-consuming. I was recently talking to a man who needed to change his job, but it meant moving to another part of the country. He explained that he couldn't move and therefore couldn't take up new employment. Apparently, his wife had a best friend who lived locally and refused to move away from her.

I could sympathise with the wife, but felt that something was wrong where a friendship outside the marriage prevented a wife from even considering her husband's needs. Just the other day I heard about a marriage of 20 years breaking up because the wife had left to go and live with her best friend.

These sort of problems are usually caused because we bring unresolved baggage from the past into the relationship. If such things go unrecognised it will foul one relationship after another, which is why the first step in healing is recognition – facing up to reality.

Paul was Timothy's mentor and the letters he received from Paul are full of advice for a young church leader. In one of the letters he tells Timothy to watch his life and his doctrine closely, because in that way he will save both himself and his hearers.[10] Jeremiah tells us bluntly that the heart is deceitful above all things and beyond cure.[11] One of the best antidotes to getting things wrong in a relationship or any other situation is to work courageously at knowing ourselves – both our strengths and weaknesses. Then, where necessary, to seek healing and resolution for the past hurts that we are still carrying with us.

I remember praying with a couple of friends who had hit a very rocky patch. One of the women felt that she was giving and giving in the relationship and it wasn't being sufficiently appreciated by her friend. The friend felt she was behaving quite normally and that she wasn't being ungrateful. It turned out that this had been a behaviour pattern for the first lady, who all her life felt had unappreciated. She had spent her life rescuing her family and in her mind they had just taken her for granted. In this new relationship she was repeating the same pattern of giving and helping and once again was feeling unappreciated. Until this pattern was brought into the open and recognised as being unhealthy there was little hope that the relationship would ever flourish.

Self-awareness won't guarantee success in our relationships, but it will help us to build in some checks and balances. For instance, it may just be something as simple as a difference in personality. If you know that you are inclined to introversion and not sharing your thoughts, you can make a decision to speak out. Or at least you can ask your friend to remind you to do so. Or maybe you are particularly sensitive to criticism? Then practice receiving it in a positive manner, rather than responding with anger or becoming the tearful victim. Knowing oneself is the first step in healing and making changes. But it takes work, courage and determination. Benjamin Franklin said that three things are extremely hard: steel, diamonds and knowing oneself.

Self-awareness leads us to seek healing where it is needed and, once the past wounds begin to heal up, then we can move naturally into forgiving those who we imagine have hurt us. Then we can repent for those ungodly ways of protecting ourselves from more hurt and finally we can begin the work of changing our unhealthy and sometimes ungodly responses.

Though self-awareness is vital and healing may be necessary, it is more important to remember how the passage in Ecclesiastes ends. It starts with two friends together but it ends with the words, *"A chord of three strands is not quickly broken."* The writer knew that friendship based on a mutual love for God and respect for His laws is more likely to be wholesome and enduring. I have no doubt that it is that third strand, the presence of God, which has kept my relationships strong through the years. Friendship is definitely high on the list of things for which I want to give God thanks.

Endnotes:

1. Genesis 2:18
2. 2 Samuel 1:25-26
3. Ecclesiastes 4:9-12
4. Piers Morgan interview with Oprah Winfrey, CNN, January 18, 2011.
5. Ephesians 4:15
6. Proverbs 27:6
7. Proverbs 27:17
8. Strobel, Lee, The Case for Christ, Zondervan, 1998.
9. Strobel, Lee, The Case for a Creator, Zondervan, 2004.
10. 1 Timothy 4:16
11. Jeremiah 17:9

12
Thankfulness

I live with a man whose glass is half full, whereas mine is usually half empty. So for me to be thankful in all circumstances is a discipline. Soon after coming into the things of the Spirit in Chile we had to find somewhere new to live. We had been renting a house high up on the side of a hill. There were 79 steps to the front door and we rejoiced in keeping fit, until we had an earthquake and the water was cut off for about three weeks and we had to fetch it from a well about three blocks away. It was hard to praise God as we struggled up those steps with buckets of water. So when the owners wanted the house back we were excited at the thought of living somewhere without so many steps! But there were very few houses on the market and as we searched the local paper we began to get desperate.

One afternoon I was standing in a queue for bread when I overheard a woman talking to a friend about a house that was coming on the market. I thought I knew where it was so I immediately drove around to see the house. It was charming, but strangely there was no "for sale" notice outside. However, when I told the family they were anxious to see it. So that evening we packed the girls in the car and drove around so that we could all take a look. Whilst we were peering over the gate, with the girls squealing with delight, the owner came out of the house. We asked him if the house was up for sale and he said absolutely not. He was an Admiral in the Navy and was stationed in the port of Valparaiso and was not considering a move. So we left our name and telephone number just in case and we got in the car feeling very despondent.

"Well," said my irritatingly cheerful husband, "we will just have to thank God!"

"No way!" shouted the girls. "We loved the house!"

But David was determined that we praise God anyway. So we began to sing choruses and thank God that He knew what He was doing, and we declared our trust in His unfailing love and that whatever His plan, it was for the best for us.

The amazing thing was that we were in that house within the week. Apparently, the day after we saw the house the Admiralty called the owner to offer him a new posting with immediate effect. They rang us and asked if we would be able to move in so that the house was not left empty while he explored this new turn of events. After living in that charming little house for three months, rent free, we were able to buy it on behalf of the Diocese for the equivalent of £3,000. It was a good lesson in learning to praise God whatever the circumstances.

The seventies in Chile was not an easy time. First we had a communist regime, with the shortages, queues and unrest, then there was the military coup with curfews and nightly gun battles – even once or twice just outside our house – so sometimes praise was the last thing on my mind. Realising my struggles a friend gave me a notice to put on the window sill by my draining board, knowing I would read it several times a day. On it were printed just two words: "Hallelujah Anyway". It was a good reminder, though occasionally I said it through gritted teeth!

Over the years I have discovered more and more the power in praise. It lifts my spirit, it refocuses me, it puts me in a right place with God. But in hard times it doesn't come naturally and one may even feel a little bit hypocritical. Several thoughts have been helpful to me.

First of all, Jesus didn't thank God for suffering or sin. To thank God for the recent earthquakes in Haiti or Chile would seem to lack integrity. "I don't understand the suffering in the world, but You are still God Almighty and You are still deserving of my praise" would be a more appropriate response. After all, Paul encourages us to, *"Give thanks in all circumstances,"*[1] not *for* all circumstances.

Jesus was indignant at the money changers who were abusing the temple. He certainly didn't give God thanks for them. Sometimes outrage is a more appropriate response. But whatever happens to us or to those we love, God is still God. And He is still good. A recurring song in the Old Testament was one about the goodness and love of God. *"God is good and His love endures forever"*[2] they would sing. It is such an easy refrain and I have found it really helps me to focus on the One who created me and loves me so generously.

It will always take discipline to thank God in all circumstances, especially in those difficult times. But Paul doesn't just tell us to do it, he goes on to remind us that it is God's will for us.[3] Gratitude is not an optional extra. It's not just something we do when everything in the garden is rosy. It's expected of us, because we are adopted children of the Most High God and have the immense privilege of being able to come into His presence and call Him "Abba", Father. And yes, I might be a person who tends to look on the negative side, but in that case it will just take a little bit more discipline to obey the injunction to be thankful whatever is happening to me, or around me.

Old habits die hard and new ones are difficult to make, but I have found that the more I work at something the more it eventually becomes an habitual way of life. It is rather comforting to read in Hebrews that praise is a sacrifice,[4] which means it will cost me something. It may mean some form of hardship, but when it is done out of love there is something joyful about it.

I remember when we were first married actually darning David's socks when I hate sewing. And also making a fruit cake when I would rather have had a sponge. Then I remember the sacrifices my parents made so that we could have a good education. They did it because they loved us. Then I remember how God so loved the world that He gave His own Son to die for us. He made a massive sacrifice for us. So whatever we feel, wherever we are, whatever our age or health, it doesn't seem too much to ask that out of gratitude we give something back to God.

People all over the world have embraced Matt and Beth Redmans' song, mentioned previously, *Blessed be Your Name*, which contains the words, "On the road marked with suffering, though there is pain in the offering, blessed be Your name." It is popular because people everywhere identify with the idea of praise being a sacrifice and at times, even painful. But it is an offering which is required of us and pleases God's heart.

It must have been a sacrifice for Habakkuk to praise God when his country lay in ruins, but his song has lifted the hearts of millions down through the ages:

"Though the fig-tree does not bud and there are no grapes on

the vines, though the olive crop fails and fields produce no food, though there are no sheep in the pen and no cattle in the stalls [this was a real recession!], yet I will rejoice in the Lord, I will be joyful in God my Saviour."⁵ The NIV Study Bible calls this one of the strongest affirmations of faith in all Scripture. God loves faith and when we give Him thanks and praise, even when times are tough, it demonstrates our trust in His unfailing love.

Remembering also helps me. Remembering the ways in which God has provided for us, protected us, and given us the privilege of playing a small part in His purposes. It would be easy to feel a little depressed with the limitations that accompany aging, except that living as we do in the cyber age enables us to keep in touch with many of the people who have played an important part in our lives down through the ages, but who like us are not either wealthy enough or fit enough to travel. Keeping in touch causes one to remember.

The Jews were always encouraged to remember all the wonderful things God had done for them and to pass them on to their children. Only yesterday I sat talking in the local coffee shop with an elderly gentleman. His health is not great and we could easily have sat and bemoaned our aches and pains. But instead he told me of the many times God had met his needs in the most amazing ways. It lifted my heart and once again caused me to be thankful for God's tender concern for His children.

I have never been able to hold a tune on my own. My husband once rudely described me as someone who "lives in A flat and has lost the key!" However, I enjoy music and we have had the privilege of worshipping in a church with an amazing worship band. Soul Survivor has produced many young worship leaders and many of the new songs being sung in churches around the world. Their band is probably one of the best in the country, so it is easy to spend half an hour non-stop praising God in that environment.

But what about the small churches where the worship group is not so good and half the congregation would rather not sing "those choruses" anyway? It is very difficult in that sort of situation to keep focused on praising God and difficult sometimes not to be groaning inside and wishing it would end soon. First, I have found that It helps me if I keep focused on the One I am worshipping and not the people who may be leading. Secondly, I find it best to think about the words I am singing and not the sound. And it helps me to remember that in any case, my worship, in comparison to the angels and what is going on in Heaven, is all pretty pathetic. Of course, we should give the best we can give, but nothing is ever going to be as good as it will be one day.

Then, of course, I have to remind myself that praising God is a sacrifice. It is good if it costs me something. However, having said that, I have great sympathy for those who are unhappy with the way the sung part of worship is conducted in their local church. But as my husband constantly reminds me, we go to give something to God not just to receive from Him.

Our greatest enemy is our consumerist society. Whatever our age, we have all bought into it to some extent. The attitude then is, "Does this satisfy me? Does this do anything for me?" Sacrifice doesn't seem to be in vogue and I wonder if anyone these days is as enthralled as I was by the missionary biographies and the huge sacrifices made by some of those early pioneers to places like China and Africa. I was so inspired by their lives that they made me long to reach for more. Thankfulness may take discipline and it may be a sacrifice, but when we embrace it we will discover a powerful tool.

Throughout my life I have struggled with anxiety. Maybe I have too active an imagination. Whatever the reason, I have prayed and looked for ways of overcoming it and of all the tools I have used the one that helps the most is this one: to turn my mind to praising God and thanking Him. When I do this, I find that my negative emotions begin to lose their control over me. We all long to have more victory in our lives over attitudes that are not glorifying to God. Praise may be one of the keys to this victory.

When King Jehoshaphat, King of Judah, went to battle against Moab and Ammon, he received a word from the Lord that the battle was not theirs but God's. They just had to stand firm and see the deliverance that the Lord would give them. Jehoshaphat's response was to set men in front of the army to praise God for the splendour of His holiness saying, *"Give thanks to the Lord for His love endures forever."*[6] The battle was won without the Jews having to raise a finger. God fought for them as they sang His praises.

When King Solomon had finished building the temple he brought the ark into it and all the musicians and the people gathered, with one voice, gave God praise and thanks and sang, *"'God is good and his love endures forever.' Then the temple of the Lord was filled with a cloud and the priests could not perform their service because of it, for the glory of the Lord filled the temple of God."*[7]

That's just a foretaste of Heaven. One day we will see Jesus face to face, then praise and thanksgiving will come naturally to our lips. Meanwhile, it may take some effort and discipline.

One of my greatest causes for thanksgiving has been the fact that my friends have grown older at the same pace as myself. We have been able to comfort one another over the losses, laugh together about some of the more comical problems we've faced, and give each other advice if we have found a resolution to one of the difficulties of old age. Having gone past the middle stage of life and spent several years in the OAP stage, I thought it might be appropriate to share a few crumbs of wisdom I have picked up on the way.

Endnotes:

1. 1 Thessalonians 5:18
2. 2 Chronicles 5:13
3. 1 Thessalonians 5:18
4. Hebrews 13:15
5. Habakkuk 3:17-18
6. 2 Chronicles 20:21
7. 2 Chronicles 5:13-14

13
Growing Older

David and I have both been fortunate to have lived very full and exciting lives. Our retirement has been different, but equally eventful. Now we are forced to face the prospect of old age – the golden years. I have often wondered why old age is so called, but I realise that the autumn of our lives, like the autumn itself, has some glorious golden hues. The trees and bushes prepare to lose their leaves and nature gets ready to sleep the winter away until it re-awakens to spring and new life.

I would like to think that I will face the future with good sense and courage. But it is easy to feel depressed by the losses that are becoming an inevitable part of life. In the monologue from Shakespeare's *As You Like It*, Jaques paints old age in very dreary terms:

All the world's a stage,
And all the men and women merely players:

They have their exits and their entrances;
And one man in his time plays many parts,
His acts being seven ages. At first the infant...

And so it continues until the rather depressing bit comes:

The sixth age shifts
Into the lean and slipper'd pantaloon,
With spectacles on nose and pouch on side,
His youthful hose, well saved, a world too wide
For his shrunk shank; and his big manly voice,
Turning again toward childish treble, pipes
And whistles in his sound. Last scene of all,
That ends this strange eventful history,
Is second childishness and mere oblivion,
Sans teeth, sans eyes, sans taste, sans everything.[1]

I prefer to limit my thoughts to the words of St Paul:

"For I have learned to be content in whatever the circumstances. I know what it is to be in need and I know what it is to have plenty. I have learned the secret of being content in any and every situation, whether well fed or hungry, whether living in plenty or in want. I can do everything through him who gives me strength."[2]

And in the same letter he writes that for him to die is gain and to live is Christ.[3] Paul sees the positive side of both.

It is natural to have some qualms about growing older. We ask ourselves questions such as, "Will we stay healthy? ... will our finances be adequate? ... will we still have friends?" And then there are the niggling little fears about such things as getting out of the bath, keeping clean and fresh and of course, for women, "who will pluck my whiskers?" My desire is to grow old gracefully, but how? I have found some tips to help us face up to the fact that our bodies and therefore our lives are changing and in some ways it is downhill from now on.

First, I think we must face the truth. Our bodies will show wear and tear, our memories will be tuned into the past more than the present, our circulation may deteriorate and we may become increasingly dependent upon others. Those are the facts and it is better to acknowledge them than live in denial. I read in the Sunday Telegraph magazine a few years ago that there is probably more displacement activity going on in people's mind about ageing than any other subject. Quite simply, no one wants to get older. We may have negotiated middle age reasonably well, but how will we deal with the years ahead?

John Lennon once said that the only thing he was afraid of was growing old. It's quite natural to have our worries, but we should also remind ourselves of the benefits. The Bible is very positive about our latter years. In the Old Testament authority was given to older people – the Elders – who had a greater experience of life. They were considered more qualified to hold positions of leadership. Moses was one of the greatest leaders the world has ever known and yet he was eighty when he led the people of Israel out of Egypt. By the time King David handed the kingdom over to Solomon Israel was a great nation. But when Solomon handed it on to Rehoboam it was not only great, but powerful and wealthy too. But Rehoboam was young and instead of listening to the Elders who could guide him in his new responsibilities, he turned to his young friends. Consequently, he made disastrous decisions that caused his subjects to rebel and left the kingdom divided.

The New Testament story of Jesus begins with two people, Simeon and Anna, who recognised the baby Jesus to be the Messiah.[4] In fact Anna, we are told, was very old and Simeon felt his life's work was done: *"Lord, now let your servant depart in peace."*[5] Peter, in his famous Pentecost sermon, quotes from Joel who had prophesied that the old men would dream dreams. They would be aware of God speaking to them. God clearly doesn't stop speaking to us because we are getting older.

So the Bible is very positive about old age and whenever we may feel a little gloomy about the prospect we may comfort ourselves with that. But in one sense that is being *re-active*, which means we are reacting to the situation we find ourselves in instead of being *pro-active* and preparing for the future. A few years ago I read some good advice for the middle years and it could equally be said of old age:

"I have some useful tips on how to cope with middle age. Stop saying how expensive things are – terribly ageing. If you have rheumatism in your shoulder, say it's tendonitis. Never be photographed in colour; you may come out with a pink face like Bill Clinton's. Don't wear a baseball cap or shorts. Buy a violent yellow or orange plastic case for your spectacles (we spend a year of our lives looking for things, most of this for our spectacles). Keep a magnifying glass near any new cookery books; these are now printed on pale grey paper in pale grey ink, the page numbers cunningly concealed. It's a good idea to live in the country where looking good for one's age looks out of place. It also keeps you in touch with the cycle of birth and death and rebirth. Remember that if you have grey hair, you are invisible. The young waiter who has been so chatty and charming and for whom you have left a colossal tip won't recognise you if he sees you in the street two minutes later. There are advantages. You can hang around listening to more interesting people at parties because they can't see you..."[6]

Being pro-active means we take some time to look ahead and

take whatever sensible measures are needed to enable us to cope as well as possible with the fact of aging. Physical health is probably the one we are most concerned with. Apparently, physical maturity is reached by the time we are 18, but physical health doesn't stop at this age. Paul tells us that our bodies are the temples of the Holy Spirit and that we should therefore honour God with our bodies.[7]

Staying as healthy as possible takes discipline, persistence and understanding. We live in a very stressful and polluted world that is in not very conducive to healthy living. However, there are obvious measures we can take to help ourselves. A good diet is as important to the elderly as it is to the young. About ten years ago I decided to see a nutritionist. It was money well spent. She was very helpful and gave me some useful tips. Best of all was to sprinkle two teaspoons of linseed every day over my breakfast cereal and to cut down on the gluten in my diet. Just those two things alone completely revolutionised my digestive system. Exercise is a must, of course. Walk for 20 minutes a day if possible, but for when the weather is bad, buy a simple strider. It's the least expensive of exercise machines and doesn't put a strain on the knees. Some of my friends go to pilates classes and find that a great help. Pamela Smith has written seven rules for staying fit, fuelled and free:

1. Eat early, eat often, eat balanced, eat lean
2. Water is the beverage of champions
3. Variety is the spice of life
4. Stress is a stretch that makes you snap or makes you strong
5. Exercise is vital to wellbeing
6. Rest is the key to recharging
7. Wellness is an inside-out job[8]

But with all our care our bodies will continue deteriorating gradually. Fighting the aging process seems to me to be rather pointless and makes one look a little ridiculous. I heard of one diva who couldn't close her eyes when she slept because she had had so many face lifts. However, we should all try to look as attractive as possible, even if it is only for the sake of what others have to look at. I have met many old people who have kept themselves beautiful. Eleanor Rosevelt once said that beautiful young people were accidents of nature, but beautiful old people are works of art.

So much for our bodies. What about our minds? To stay mentally healthy we need to use our minds, even challenge them as much as possible. Besides his writing David does the crossword every day and I do the Sudoku and codeword puzzles in the newspaper. I know others who have decided to go to evening classes in computer studies or to learn another language. Of course, you can do all these things and even earn a degree, but mental health is not just to do with cleverness. You can be very clever but not very wise.

Luke tells us that Jesus was filled with wisdom.[9] Not that He studied under any famous rabbi or received a doctorate in theology. People were, in fact, amazed at Jesus' knowledge, but they didn't ask which rabbi He studied under – they just wanted to know, "Where did He get His wisdom?"[10] Knowledge is about learning facts, but wisdom is about looking at the facts and then being able to make a mature choice. So often we look at the facts then mix them with some hidden agenda of our own or with pre-conceived ideas and this doesn't lend itself to making wise choices.

When we first began attending the Soul Survivor church I had a battle in my mind when I saw youngsters of either sex coming to church with rings in very strange places. One girl had a very short T-shirt on and one could not miss seeing the ring in her navel. She had another in her lip as well as several up and down her ears. Her hair was dyed purple and she looked extraordinary. My first thought was, "What is she doing in church?" But she was going to the prayer meeting before the service and I was completely stunned when she began praying passionately for every aspect of the service. I had to rethink my attitude.

Wisdom means we will recognise when our attitudes are influenced by our preconceived ideas and hidden agendas. It also means we will be flexible and willing to change. It is being open to new ideas and other people's points of view. I remember going to a prayer meeting in the early days of our time in Chile with pastors and church leaders from other denominations, among which were some Pentecostal pastors. I was expecting an orderly time of intercession with each of us taking our turn to pray. I was almost knocked backwards by the volume of noise which suddenly erupted in the room.

These men and women hit the floor and began to cry out to God with one voice. I very nearly walked out. Afterwards I complained to David that I felt it was a bit out of order. But he thought that there had been more power per square foot than could be found in most Anglican churches. That gave me some food for thought and made me realise that if we were to survive in Chile, I was going to have to become a bit more flexible.

It's not just our preconceived ideas which need to be challenged, but also the way we cling to things which have been meaningful and precious to us. Often they have to give way in order to allow new things to have room to grow and flourish. It is especially difficult if we have had an investment in things from the past which were wholesome. In a church, growth can easily be stymied by older folk holding on to support for a society or meeting which they have been involved in for years, and in so doing tying up money, time and room which could be used for the "new thing" that God is wanting to do.

Change gets more difficult the older we get, unless, of course, we have been making changes all our lives and have stayed flexible. One of the keys to remaining open-minded is to sort out the difference between *culture* and *values*. Values don't change, but culture does. We tend to muddle these two and then we demand that the younger generation stay with our culture. For example, worship is often a bone of contention in many churches. Worshiping together is a priority for any Christian and for any church. However, the way we worship is all to do with culture. The old tend to like it quiet and with the old hymns they know by heart, and the young like it loud, with a strong beat and with a new song most weeks. It is worth remembering that worship is an essential value, how we do it is a cultural preference.

Another core value is evangelism. We want people to know Jesus, especially the next generation – not least because the Church will die without it. So let's be flexible enough to make the necessary changes, so that the young will feel at home and have room to express themselves.

So if we are to stay mentally healthy we need to keep our brains active, recognise when we are acting out of our own personal and often hidden agenda, stay flexible and accept that the way we do things may often have to change. But another aspect of life needs to be considered and that is the social side. We are born and created out of the community of the Trinity and are not made for "aloneness". As we get older it is more difficult to make new friends, therefore we have to nurture the ones we already have. David is an extrovert and therefore it's no effort for him to keep in regular touch with friends old and new. His day is not complete unless he has met or chatted with someone besides myself. I am more of an introvert and therefore it is harder to involve others. But nevertheless, I know that I still need others and I can't expect to leave it all up to my friends to make the effort to keep in touch.

It is also important to make the effort to listen to our friends and to be patient even when we don't always agree with them. If we don't listen, we soon won't have any friends. We have to learn to receive as well as give to our friends and relatives. I have always found it easier to give than to receive, but I remind myself of how depressing it was when I would buy something I thought my mother would like, only to have her to put it in a cupboard with hardly a glance, or even occasionally give it away to someone else. She was amazingly generous herself, but could be so unthinking in the way she received from others.

Our families will love us more if we keep our visits reasonably brief. Someone has said that visitors are like fish – after three days they smell! Our children and grandchildren have their lives to live and it is not always convenient for them to give us the time we would love to have. It is not that they don't love us, it is just the fraught and hectic world in which we live. One of the ways of enjoying and keeping up with grandchildren is through Facebook. I can see their latest photos, know who their friends are and what they have been doing. Neither David nor I have ever been particularly interested in football, but with ten grandsons in the family it has been important to, at least, have some idea of what team they support and how it is doing.

Then, of course, we have to strive to keep emotionally healthy. Because loss is part of growing older we need to remind ourselves that suppressing our emotions is not healthy. Just the other day I read an article entitled "Keeping a poker face is a bad deal."[11]

Daniel Beal, who is a professor of psychology, said that it takes energy to suppress emotions, so it is not surprising that workers who remain neutral show greater levels of burn-out. One of the joys of contemporary friends is that they understand better than any what we are feeling when we suffer yet another loss, whatever type of loss it might be. All we need to do is to ring a friend up or even email them and tell them that we need to tell someone how we feel. Emotionally healthy people have learned to express their feelings appropriately. In other words, not suppressing them, but neither expressing them boringly to whomsoever will listen.

One of the things I have always wanted and tried to do was to live peacefully with everyone, as much as I can, especially with my family. Issues do arise, but we need to resolve them as quickly as possible. It's not good for our health, emotionally, physically or spiritually, to carry resentment, bitterness or unforgiveness around. I remember a man once telling me the story of his elderly mother who had developed cancer. When he visited her in hospital she was very poorly and the doctor said that there was nothing they could do. When he went home to tell his wife she immediately said that if that was the case, he needed to ask his mother's forgiveness for causing her so much worry when he left home in his late teens without saying goodbye or even making contact for many years. So he went back to the hospital and asked his mother to forgive him, whereupon she asked him to forgive her also for having made home such an uncomfortable place that had made him want to run away. It was a very healing time for them both, but what was more extraordinary was that by the end of the week she was discharged from the hospital and well enough to go home.

As already mentioned, we have to learn to face loss. Losses will increase with age and we may as well adapt to them as soon as possible and learn to deal with them in a healthy manner. There may be the painful loss of friends and family. People die – it is a fact of life. The closer people are to us the harder it is to handle and we will mourn their loss. But that's how it should be. It may be the loss of our own abilities or those of our spouse. David was an excellent table tennis player in his time and though he had little practice, he could still beat his sons-in-law. Every year two of them would decide that this year one of them would beat the champion. Even into middle age David managed to hold on to the title. But then the day came when one of them triumphed over him. "The king is dead, long live the king," we all chanted. But I remember feeling slightly sad at what the victory meant. It is right and proper to grieve our losses. So none of us should be alarmed if we feel emotional about what will be next.

The other day David and I were visiting some friends who had sadly had to go into care due to increasing immobility. One of them confessed that she found it very difficult to be "spiritual" without any Christian fellowship in the "home". I offered to take my friend some books to read, but she confessed to finding it even difficult to concentrate. It made me think about keeping myself spiritually healthy and to put some effort into it while I am still able. Once our mental capacity begins to fade or our health deteriorates, it becomes increasingly difficult to maintain the vital links which have helped us, such as church activities, reading helpful books and the stimulation of a Bible study group.

So how can we help ourselves? A friend older than myself tells me that she tries to learn verses of Scripture so that if she was ever imprisoned without her Bible she would have the Word of God stored in her heart. Well, in once sense old age can be like an imprisonment! One's abilities have faded and we may find ourselves imprisoned in a decrepit body that will no longer do what we would like it to. So perhaps, as we look towards old age, we should start repeating Scripture to ourselves, picking verses that would be of particular help to us. Let's learn to pray some of the old prayers that would be easy to repeat in the night watches. When I am awake at night (which I find these days that I tend to be), I often repeat the Lord's prayer or the 23rd Psalm. I go through the Lord's prayer line by line, using it as a basis for wider prayer. Or I use The Jesus Prayer: "Lord Jesus Christ, Son of God have mercy on me, a sinner. Lord Jesus Christ, Son of God..." etc.

I have certain books which have blessed me over the years and when I need a spiritual lift I will take one down and, like an old friend, read it for comfort and refreshment. And we must not forget that Jesus left us with the sacraments for our benefit. These days many churches seem to have lost the importance of taking communion. It is either tagged on to the end of a service, rather like an afterthought, or it is celebrated so infrequently that it can be missed for months. I tease my friend, Prue Bedwell, because she has a few high Church tendencies. We tell her that she is more "up the candle" than we are. But I have appreciated her desire to take communion even when we have been travelling. When we travel with our husbands then of course we have our own private chaplain with us and on a Sunday, David will lead us in an informal communion service. But sometimes on our own at home we have celebrated the Lord's Supper as an "agape" – a love feast. As we grow older it might be more difficult to attend the communion at church on a regular basis, but most church leaders are prepared to send someone to visit who will bring elements already blessed at the church and celebrate privately.

I can't sing a note in tune, but there are hymns which I can remember from when I first became a Christian. At Bible college I especially loved singing the song, "Turn your eyes upon Jesus, look full in His wonderful face and the things of earth will grow strangely dim in the light of His glory and grace." We would sing it as a form of Grace on a Friday evening, when we had all returned from our practical work, visiting and taking services in care homes. These words come back to me more readily than some of the newer songs that we sing in church today.

I loved something I read on the Internet the other day, which many of us will remember from Sunday School or family services. It was shared by an elderly gentleman of 92.

"A church in Atlanta honoured one of its senior pastors who had been retired many years. He was 92 at that time and I wondered why the church even bothered to ask the old gentleman to preach at that age. After a warm welcome and introduction of the speaker, and as the applause quieted down, he rose from his high back chair and walked slowly, with great effort and a sliding gait to the podium. Without a note or written paper of any kind he placed both hands on the pulpit to steady himself and then quietly and slowly he began to speak...

'When I was asked to come here today and talk to you, your pastor asked me to tell you what was the greatest lesson ever learned in my 50-odd years of preaching. I thought about it for a few days and boiled it down to just one thing that made the most difference in my life and sustained me through all my trials. The one thing that I could always rely on when tears and heartbreak and pain and fear and sorrow paralysed me ... the only thing that would comfort was this verse:

"Jesus loves me this I know.
For the Bible tells me so.
Little ones to Him belong,
we are weak but He is strong.

Yes, Jesus loves me,
The Bible tells me so."'

Another pastor stated, "I always noticed that it was the adults who chose the children's hymn, *Jesus Loves Me* (for the children, of course) during a hymn sing, and it was the adults who sang the loudest because I could see they knew it the best. Here for you now is a Senior version of *Jesus Loves Me*:

Jesus loves me, this I know,
Though my hair is white as snow
Though my sight is growing dim,
Still He bids me trust in Him.

(Chorus)
YES, JESUS LOVES ME. YES, JESUS LOVES ME.
YES, JESUS LOVES ME, FOR THE BIBLE TELLS ME SO.

Though my steps are oh, so slow,
With my hand in His I'll go
On through life, let come what may,
He'll be there to lead the way.

Chorus

When the nights are dark and long,
In my heart He puts a song.
Telling me in words so clear,
Have no fear, for I am near.

Chorus

When my work on earth is done,

And life's victories have been won.

He will take me home above,

Then I'll understand His love.

Chorus

I love Jesus, does He know?

Have I ever told Him so?

Jesus loves to hear me say,

That I love Him every day."

Finally, as we face the future, all we need to know is that Jesus loves me! But old age is not the end of the story. There is more to come.

Endnotes:

1. Shakespeare, William, As You Like It, Act II, Scene 7.

2. Philippians 4:11-13

3. Philippians 1:22

4. Luke 2:25-38

5. Luke 25:29

6. Cleave, Maureen, Sunday Telegraph article, 18-02-2001.

7. 1 Corinthians 6:19

8. Smith, Pamela M., Food for Life, Siloam, 1997.

9. Luke 2:40

10. Matthew 13:54

11. Daily Telegraph newspaper article

14
More Glory

I have read many books about times of revival, but never hoped we would be caught up in one. However, in the early 1970's in Chile, when we were under a military regime there was an outpouring in one of our churches. David was the Diocesan Bishop at the time and the pastor of the church came to him to invite him to a baptism down by the river.

"Why not in the church?" asked David.

"We don't have enough water," said the pastor.

Apparently there had been a mini-revival in his church and men and women were coming to Christ spontaneously, so that eventually they had about a hundred people to be baptised.

The military were keeping everything under tight control so we had to get permission to have such a big meeting. Soldiers were sent to guard the bridge near where the baptisms were taking place and they watched with fascination while some hundred people, wrapped in white sheets were either sprinkled with water as they stood at the side of the river or, in the deep, were plunged right under. It was a wonderful sight and afterwards several hundred of us had a praise party. We sang and danced and the soldiers stood spellbound as the young people danced around them.

We never thought we would see such sights again, but more was to come. During the eighties many people were coming to the church in Chorleywood for training and so we began to end those days with a celebration. These grew and grew and eventually had to be stopped because the crowds were becoming dangerous. They were sitting in every corner of the building. We used to joke and say they were even in the broom cupboard. But if there had been a fire – apart from the fire of Heaven – we would have been in trouble. However, while they lasted they were wonderful times. People were healed, blessed and set ablaze for God. We could hardly believe that God had allowed us to be part of such an outpouring.

Just the other day I walked out of church with an elderly friend who has the beginnings of dementia. But she knew me and she remembered some of those times. "They were good days, weren't they?" she said to me. I had to agree with her. God graciously allowed us to live through some of the most exciting times in the church's recent history. Leaders' days were started and once again the church became packed with people coming from all over the country to enjoy the presence of God. It was towards the end of the '80s that David began some weeks away for leaders and some of their congregation. These became so full it was obvious a bigger venue was needed. The West of England showground was chosen as a good place to have a church away week where we could invite whoever wanted to join us.

Those early years were very special as nearly the whole of our church moved *en masse* to Shepton Mallet for a week in the summer and hosted a few thousand people. Everywhere one went our folk were serving coffee, working with children, praying with people, cleaning the toilets and serving in every other way possible. It was a remarkable sight. New Wine, as it was called, has since grown in a most phenomenal manner and is now a large network of church leaders all across the country. It hosts about 30,000 people every year at show grounds in this country and has sprung up in many other countries as well. David has long retired from its leadership, but it is a joy and privilege to see younger leaders who were part of those early days at Chorleywood taking it over so enthusiastically.

It is wonderful too, to see such a great number of people getting blessed by God, but recently I have been reminded that though we rejoice to see the crowds, numbers are not what it is all about. We have a tendency to measure success by numbers and God has had to remind me on several occasions that that is not how He measures it.

Some years ago I was invited to lead a conference in America and I set off with my friend, Prue Bedwell, expecting to receive the usual American hospitality. Our first shock was that there was no one there to meet us. It had been a long trip and for us it was midnight and we were past being ready for bed. Our hosts turned up an hour late having stopped to have a meal on the way. I struggled with some difficult feelings during the final stretch of our journey to our destination. But worse was to come. On the way our hosts explained that their organisation was going through some difficulties and they had not got around to advertising the conference in the normal way, so they were sorry but only 13 people were coming. They had realised that they should have cancelled the conference, but they had left it too late. I was speechless.

When we arrived at our accommodation, again they were not quite ready for their guests and we were left another half an hour in a hallway sitting on our bags, while our new hosts finished decorating our room! By this time it was three in the morning, our time, and I couldn't believe it was happening to us. When we eventually dropped into bed I was too tired to pray, but as I shut my eyes a few words came into my mind: "God offends the mind to reveal the heart." It was something I had heard quoted a few months previously.

The next morning I took off to walk around a nearby lake and asked God to speak to me. I felt humbled by what He showed me about my heart. Why had I expected to be treated in any special way? Where had I gone wrong that I was so dependent on numbers for my sense of value? All I could do was to repent and ask God to forgive me. In fact, we spent three days with a receptive and interesting group of people and it proved to be a very worthwhile time.

A good friend of ours, Alf Cooper, who is a missionary in Chile, recently came to stay and was on fire with the joy of the Lord. Apparently he had paid a visit to a church in Colombia where he met a pastor called Jorge Rodriguez. Jorge had been a pastor in Columbia for a several years, but became alarmed at the number of church leaders being shot dead by the drug barons when they refused to pay protection money, so he decided to move to Miami. While there he felt God speak to him: "If I want you dead, Jorge, I could arrange for it here – go home."

So he packed up and went back to Columbia. But now he didn't have a church, so how was he to start one? He read the latest books on church planting, studied church growth and prayed, but then again he felt God speak to him: "Jorge, don't seek numbers, seek my presence." So that's what he did. Day after day he would lie on the carpet in the sitting room and seek God's presence. Now that man leads a church of many thousands. During the services he encourages the people to call out for the presence of God. And when *el nube* or "the cloud" of God descends many wonderful things begin to happen – people are healed, set free and blessed. Our friend Alf had come away not just blessed himself, but convinced that he too must seek God's presence.

I know that God is with us, but there is no doubt that we can have more – more of His glory. We need those times of special visitation. Down through the ages we read of men and women who have sought God – men like Wesley, D.L. Moody and Evan Roberts; saints who spent time seeking God and saw His glory come. Prayer is the key to God's presence and, of course, to manifestations of His power. A book that has inspired me greatly is, *Fresh Wind, Fresh Fire* by Jim Cymbala, pastor of the Brooklyn Tabernacle. I have read it more than once. He has a church of many thousands, but the most important meeting of the week is the Tuesday prayer meeting. He writes,

"God had formed a core of people who wanted to pray, who believed that nothing was too big for God to handle. No matter what roadblock we faced, no matter what attack came against us, no matter how wild the city became in the late seventies – as cocaine arrived on top of heroin, and then crack cocaine on top of that – God could still change people and deliver them from evil. He was building His Church in a tough neighbourhood and as long as people kept calling out for His blessing and help, He had fully committed Himself to respond."[1]

Cymbala tells the story of his oldest daughter, Chrissy, who at sixteen, strayed away from God and her family. There were many nights when her parents had no idea where she was. This tragic state of affairs went on for more than two years. Both he and his wife were distraught. He prayed continually and called out to God on her behalf. Then at one Tuesday evening prayer meeting, a young woman in the church sent a note up to the pastor on which she had written: "Pastor Cymbala, I feel impressed that we should stop the meeting and all pray for your daughter." So that is exactly what they did, and he writes,

"There arose a groaning, a sense of desperate determination, as if to say, 'Satan you will not have this girl. Take your hands off her – she's coming back.' I was overwhelmed. The force of that vast throng calling on God almost literally knocked me over ... Thirty-two hours later on Thursday morning, as I was shaving, Carol [his wife] suddenly burst through the door, her eyes wide. 'Go downstairs,' she blurted. 'Chrissy's here.'"

When Chrissy saw her father she fell to her knees asking for his and God's forgiveness and then she asked who had been praying for her, because in the middle of Tuesday night God had woken her and shown her that she was heading towards a dark abyss. She knew that she was on a wrong path and then she felt God wrap His arms around her saying, "I still love you." Chrissy came back home. She then went to Bible college and eventually became a pastor's wife and now has three children.

God loves to see us so desperate for His presence that we will spend time crying out to Him, because we know that *only His presence* will bring the blessing we so badly need. It was in the late '80s that my husband found himself so busy he knew that he wasn't spending enough time with God, so he decided to call a prayer meeting. He told the church it was prayer for revival, but in his heart he knew it was mainly for his own survival.

He said that he would be in the church lounge every morning at 7.00am and anyone was free to join him. They could come every day, twice a week, or even once a week. But whether there was someone there or not, he would be there.

So we began the best and most important meeting of the week. Every morning we gathered for 45 minutes. There was no great organisation to it. We would have a stack of Bibles on the table and a notice which said what passage we were reading. We would read the Bible for ten minutes, then share what God might have been saying to us through it, and finally we would pray. Standing, kneeling, sitting, walking, stretched out on the floor, crying, being silent or calling out to God, we were totally free to wait on God however He led us. At 7.45am David would close with the Lord's Prayer and everyone would make their way to work or home to their breakfast. I am not a morning person and it was very hard to discipline myself to go every morning, but when we eventually left the church that was the meeting I missed the most. And as I look back at all that God was doing in our midst, I am sure it was the result of that daily prayer meeting.

Prayer demonstrates our dependence on God. To see more of His glory we have to know without a shadow of a doubt that, "Without Him we can do nothing!" And we have to grow smaller while He grows bigger. That is how it was for John the Baptist: *"I must decrease and he must increase,"*[2] he said. We belong to an upside down kingdom where the way to up is down. Jesus made this clear just before the Last Supper, when He took off His outer garment and tied a towel around His waist and washed His disciples' feet. He then said to them, "I have set you an example that you should do as I have done for you."[3] This was one of His last opportunities to pass on the values of the kingdom to men who were to be the founders of a worldwide movement. The values of this movement would be very different from the ones they would meet in the world. Humble dependence is the only way we will know the presence of God and see His glory.

Paul longed to be strong and be rid of his thorn in the flesh, but God spoke to him clearly and said, *"My grace is sufficient for you, for my power is made perfect in weakness."* Therefore, Paul writes, *"I delight in weaknesses, in insults, in hardships, in persecutions, in difficulties. For when I am weak, then I am strong."*[4] And again Paul writes about keeping our treasure in clay pots. *"But we have this treasure in jars of clay to show that this all-surpassing power is from God and not from us."*[5] God loves humility and He sees weakness as an opportunity to show forth more of His glory. It is only too easy to get sucked into our celebrity culture and to look for the next superstar on the Christian scene, or the latest gimmick which will enable our church to become a super-church. Good teaching is important and big churches can inspire others, but in the end it's only the presence of God that counts. Nothing else does.

Since that day in 1954, when I asked Jesus into my life, I have been privileged to see glimpses of His glory. But there is more yet to come. Paul encourages us to *"fix our eyes not on what is seen but on what is unseen, for what is seen is temporary, but what is unseen is eternal."*[6] The realisation that everything in this life is temporary comes with age! Getting older definitely focuses the mind on our future destination. I feel that I fit the description in Zechariah where he calls the people of God, *"prisoners of hope"*.[7] I am a prisoner to the hope of Eternal Life. It is easy to be shaken by the happenings in the world and to grow despondent, but somehow as I shut my eyes at night I know that I cannot escape the hope that is within me. I am gloriously a prisoner to it. I would drown without it.

Death is inevitable. No one will escape it unless Jesus returns first. However, to talk about it does seem a little macabre. But we should talk about our future glory and prepare ourselves for that.

I think about death as a little like going on holiday. Some holidays are taken quite near to home and they are easy to reach. For some of us, it may be a quick, fairly painless crossing. But for others it may be a longer and more difficult journey.

We try to visit our friends in Chile every year. The journey is horrendous. First there is the anxiety about getting to the airport on time, taking into account the busyness on our roads and the many possible hold ups. Then there are the queues at the airport and the long wait for the plane to take off – usually late! The flight to Chile is very long and involves a night flight and then a wait in Buenos Aires or Sao Paulo before, at last, crossing the Andes. The last part of the journey is worth the agony. As we cross the snow capped mountains with a spectacular view of Aconcagua, the highest mountain in the southern hemisphere, my heart begins to soar. We are nearly home – at least our second home. As we begin the descent into the airport we see the Chilean vineyards and fruit farms stretching towards the coast – miles and miles of fertile land as far as the eye can see. Beyond it is the coast and I know that after another three hours we will be reaching the hills that look down into the Pacific Ocean. My heart is beating fast with excitement. The journey will soon be forgotten and only what lies ahead matters.

For some death may be drawn out, like a long journey, but it can be made less traumatic if we can keep our eyes on the place which our heart longs for. As C.S. Lewis said, "I must keep alive in myself the desire for my true country, which I shall not find until after death. I must never let it get snowed under or turned aside. I must make the main object of life to press on to that other country and to help others do the same."[8]

The more we know about that country the more excited we will be. H.S. Laird's father, a Christ-loving man lay dying. His son sat at his bedside and asked, "Dad, how do you feel?"

"Son, I feel like a little boy on Christmas Eve," he replied.

Randy Alcorn wrote a very full account of Heaven in his book by that title. In it he writes, "We should make ourselves acquainted with where we are going. How else can we become excited?" I don't think it is morbid to spend some time thinking about Eternity and what it will be like. In fact, I think we might find it very beneficial. In his book *Perelandra*, C.S. Lewis' protagonist speaks of his friend, Ransom, who has recently returned from another planet: "A man who has been in another world does not come back unchanged."[9] And Alcorn comments, "A man who gives sustained thought to another world – the Heaven where Christ is, and the resurrected Earth where we will live forever with Him – also does not remain unchanged ... He smells the banquet being prepared for him."

I have often told the story of the woman with the fork, but it is worth repeating. A lady in America was told by her doctor that she only had a few months to live, so she went home to prepare herself. She called her pastor to make arrangements for her funeral. After choosing the hymns and order of service she added, "Oh, and I want to be buried with a fork in my hand." The pastor was surprised at her peculiar request and asked why. "Well," said the lady, "I have been to many pot luck suppers and after we have finished the first course someone will come around and tell us to keep our forks for desert – and then I know that the best is yet to come. So when the people file past the open coffin (as they do in the US) I want them to see the fork and ask, 'What's with the fork?' Then I want you to tell them, 'The best is yet to come.'"

At the moment this earth is all we know and most of us earnestly fight death. We take the nasty medicine, eat the right things, take the correct amount of exercise and run to the doctor when we feel a twinge. It's normal to want to preserve life for as long as possible, but I wonder sometimes if we sound a little like people without hope. Paul makes it plain that to die is gain.

"For me to live is Christ, to die is gain. If I am to go on living in the body, this will mean fruitful labour for me. Yet what shall I choose? I do not know! I am torn between the two: I desire to depart and be with Christ, which is better by far, but it is more necessary for you that I remain in the body."[10]

How could Paul have been so keen to go to Heaven? Perhaps it was due to the time when he was caught up to the Third Heaven, which he writes about in the third person: *"And I know that this man, whether in the body or apart from the body I do not know, but God knows – was caught up to paradise. He heard inexpressible things, things that man is not permitted to tell."*[11] The experience changed him and set the course for his life. But perhaps it also gave him a taste of glory which kept his eyes continually fixed on the eternal things of God. So he was able to write to the Colossians,

"Since you have been raised to new life with Christ, set your sights on the realities of heaven, where Christ sits in the place of honour at God's right hand. Think about the things of heaven, not the things of earth. For you died to this life, and your real life is hidden with Christ in God. And when Christ, who is your life, is revealed to the whole world, you will share in all His glory."[12]

Our primary calling, as we said at the beginning of this book, is to God, and I repeat it again. We have been made in the image of our Creator and we have been made with the capacity to relate intimately with Him. One day we will see Him face to face and when we finally do, we will find ourselves in glory.

"We were all made for a person and a place. Jesus is the person. Heaven is the place. If you know Jesus, I'll be with you in that resurrected world. With the Lord we love and with the friends we cherish, we'll embark together on the ultimate adventure, in a spectacular new universe awaiting exploration and dominion. Jesus will be the centre of all things and joy will be the air we breathe. And right when we think, 'It doesn't get any better than this' — *it will*."[13]

Endnotes:

1. Cymbala, Jim, Fresh Wind, Fresh Fire, Zondervan, 2003.

2. John 3:30

3. John 13:1-17

4. 2 Corinthians 12:9-10

5. 2 Corinthians 4:7

6. 2 Corinthians 4:18

7. Zechariah 9:12

8. Lewis, C.S., Mere Christianity, HarperCollins, 2002.

9. Lewis, C.S., Perelandra, HarperCollins Entertainment, 2005.

10. Philippians 1:21-24

11. 2 Corinthians 12:3-4

12. Colossians 3:1-4 (NLT)

13. Alcorn, Randy, Heaven, Tyndale House Publishers, 2004.

About the author

Mary Pytches and her husband David were missionaries in South America for 17 years before moving back to the UK to lead St Andrew's Church, Chorleywood. They were radically impacted by the ministry of John Wimber in the early 1980s and went on to found the New Wine movement in 1989. New Wine also gave birth to Soul Survivor led by Mike Pilavachi, who began it while still a youth worker at St Andrews.

Mary has a long established teaching and counselling ministry and has written 10 books, including *Yesterday's Child*, *A Child No More*, *Dying to Change*, *Who Am I?*, *Rising Above The Storms of Life* and *Cry Freedom*.

The Road to Maturity

THE ROAD TO MATURITY IS A
SIX-WEEK DVD COURSE IDEAL FOR
INDIVIDUAL AND SMALL GROUP STUDY.

True maturity is becoming like Jesus.
As Christians we are all on the road to
maturity, but sometimes the journey is
made harder by unresolved issues from
the past which block our path. This
course is designed to uncover what
these might be, and to implement their
removal so that we may continue along
the road unhindered by the past.

The 3-DVD set comes
with an accompanying
booklet, which is also
sold separately.

IN THE PRESS:

The Road to Maturity was run by
charity Prison Fellowship at HMP
Whatton, a Category C men's
prison in Nottinghamshire. Twelve
men were chosen to take part.
"I was bowled over by their
openness and honesty in sharing
past events in their lives that
were very painful. Every one of
them met the challenges they
were presented with head on and
I know it was not easy for them",
said Vera Quick, Group Leader
for Prison Fellowship. One of the
prisoners also commented on his
experience, "The Road to Maturity
course has helped me see my past
both critically and yet without
condemnation. I know any evil
within myself can be overcome."

The Marks of Maturity

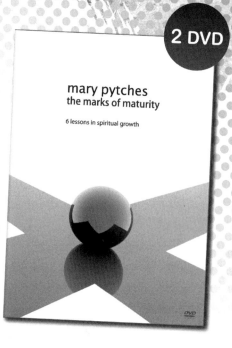

mary pytches
the marks of maturity

6 lessons in spiritual growth

FOLLOWING ON FROM THE ROAD TO MATURITY, THE MARKS OF MATURITY DVD COURSE COVERS 6 LESSONS IN SPIRITUAL GROWTH.

The process of change is fundamental to the Christian life. A continued transformation should be taking place within each of us. *The Road to Maturity* looked at blockages to maturity and how to remove them, *The Marks of Maturity* examines the indicating factors for maintaining progress. The story of the Prodigal Son, his journey away from home and his journey back, is used as a backdrop to these studies.

THE BOX SET INCLUDES SIX SESSIONS ON TWO DVDS, PLUS A COURSE BOOKLET, WHICH IS ALSO AVAILABLE TO DOWNLOAD AS A PDF FROM DISC 1.